Praise for *Seat 29B*

Easy and fun read. A lot like Steinbeck's *Travels with Charley*, but without the poodle!
>—Penny Rafferty Hamilton, author and laureate of the Colorado
>Aviation Hall of Fame and the Colorado Women's Hall of Fame

Having known Gordon Page for years, it seems like he's on the road all the time. *Seat 29B* is a must-read to get a taste of how hard travel can be, especially for an airplane enthusiast.
>—Dr. Michael W. Bertz

Drawing from his vast experience as a globe-trotting aircraft appraiser, Gordon Page has penned this anthology of high adventure (and misadventure), which will have you cringing one moment and chuckling the next. This isn't a story about the good old days of air travel!
>—Brian Richardson, aviation historian and colorful aviation character

I have followed Gordon on his adventures for many years and delighted in both the story and the storyteller. He has not, however, until now, written about the hazards of air travel—and I don't mean accidents. The travel experience has evolved from delight to a grim encounter in which every trip can feel like a contest to simply survive the assaults from fellow passengers, flight crew, agents, customs officials, and a continuous parade of marginal behavior. Gordon has captured that. He has captured the pain of travel for business but also demonstrated a clear sense of humor about the process. Sit back, relax, and enjoy the view from *Seat 29B*.
>—Paul Hinton, pilot and aviation industry professional

In *Seat 29B*, Gordon Page tells us that at one time, flying on an airliner was exciting and glamourous. Yes, it was! In my sixty-eight years of commercial airline travel, I've witnessed the change from champagne flights with menus and real linen on the tray table to, well, what you'll read about in this book. In *Seat 29B*, you'll feel the pain of being stuck in that dreaded middle seat but also be treated to some laugh-out-loud-funny incidents.
>—Steve Kelly, president, Colorado Aviation Historical Society

We can all relate to the ordeal of commercial air travel, and our family has some classic fables of our experiences with the airlines we've shared around the safety of our kitchen table. But I have to say, it is all at once refreshing, sometimes horrifying, and almost always snort-laugh humorous to read Gordon Page's accounts of his colorful life in the sky in *Seat 29B*.

—Ron Kaplan, chairman and CEO, Ohio Air
and Space Hall of Fame Museum

Gordon's latest read truly takes into account that travel is about the journey, not the destination. Each chapter of *Seat 29B* features a journey and unique encounters with cool and unusual aircraft that will have readers cringing in all the right spots.

—Paul Kraus, founder, HonyOk LLC

SEAT 29B

TRAVEL STORIES OF AN AIRPLANE FANATIC

GORDON R. PAGE

SEAT 29B
TRAVEL STORIES OF AN AIRPLANE FANATIC

iUniverse books may be ordered through booksellers or by contacting:

iUniverse
1663 Liberty Drive
Bloomington, IN 47403
www.iuniverse.com
1-800-Authors (1-800-288-4677)

Because of the dynamic nature of the Internet, any web addresses or links contained in this book may have changed since publication and may no longer be valid. The views expressed in this work are solely those of the author and do not necessarily reflect the views of the publisher, and the publisher hereby disclaims any responsibility for them.

Any people depicted in stock imagery provided by Getty Images are models, and such images are being used for illustrative purposes only.
Certain stock imagery © Getty Images.

ISBN: 978-1-6632-0492-9 (sc)
ISBN: 978-1-6632-0493-6 (e)

Library of Congress Control Number: 2020913132

Print information available on the last page.

iUniverse rev. date:07/28/2020

To my wife, Tracey, and my daughters, Glynnis and Callie.
Thanks for all your support and for not being mad when
you got sick after I got back home from a trip.

God bless the flight attendants of the world
for what you have to deal with.

Attitude is the difference between an ordeal and an adventure.

—Bob Bitchin

CONTENTS

INTRODUCTION

The seventy-foot cottonwood tree in my backyard found a water source on the day I planted it as a six-foot-tall sapling some twenty-five years ago. It quickly grew into one of the highest points in Louisville, Colorado, and it has made for a great visual landmark every time I fly over our two-story house.

It provides great shade in the summer and piles of leaves in the fall, and it was a tree of adventure for my two girls as they grew up, offering its branches for swings, for climbing, and as a haven for birds for our entire family to enjoy.

My older daughter, Glynnis, hand drew many of the birds that visited our cottonwood, and dozens of her drawings grace the Spirit of Flight Museum to this day. My younger daughter, Callie, honed her climbing skills in that tree, skills she uses often on local climbing walls.

The cottonwood has endured harsh winters, hundred-mile-per-hour winds, lightning storms, and more while standing strong near our home. It has been a good friend of our family and has given us another good friend: a great horned owl.

Hooting from the owl comes in the late evenings and early mornings from high atop the cottonwood, announcing the arrival of our friend. Just as I run out our back door to see an airplane flying over, I run to the door to greet the owl. Sure, there are superstitions that surround owls, associating them with haunting night themes and horror movies, and supposedly, they are the only creatures that can live with ghosts, but not all superstitions about owls are bad. They are also believed to bring good fortune and are a symbol of guidance and help. Maybe our owl is a bit of both, as he once showed up when our aircraft hangar supposedly had a German ghost marching around at night.

The owl also showed up the night before I was to take a trip to Russia to inspect some warbird projects for a client. It was to be my first trip back to Russia after being ripped off during a previous visit, and I was sleepless with anxiety. The hooting of the owl helped put me at ease for the trip, and little did I know that an incredibly rare Owl aircraft would be part of that trip.

It seems the great horned owl that visits our cottonwood tree likes to hoot when he senses an upcoming adventure, and I look forward to greeting him upon his arrival in the tree on nights before I travel.

People have said that my job must be one of the greatest jobs in the world and that the travel must be incredibly glamorous and fun. Sometimes it is, but sometimes I get stuck in the middle seat in the back of the plane, and the struggle of travel can be a bit overwhelming and sometimes painful.

These are some stories of my travels to chase planes around the world and some of the crazy things you can experience from seat 29B or any other seat on an airline flight—things the owl may have been trying to warn me about.

CHAPTER 1

THE GLAMOUR OF FLYING?

My job as an aircraft appraiser has taken me on adventures all over the world. I get to look at rare and collectible aircrafts in museums and private collections, and many times, I have been shown storage hangars and warehouses full of vintage aircraft projects, engines, and parts that haven't seen the light of day for years. It's a great job, one I dreamed about having when I was a kid.

Many of my clients and friends have told me how lucky I am to have a job like mine. They are right; I am lucky, and I'm thankful to get to do what I do for my day job. Many of those same people have told me that it must be incredibly glamorous to fly around the world.

Glamourous is not the word I would use to describe what I have seen and experienced in flying more than one million miles with the airlines.

At one time—say, in the 1930s—flying on an airliner *was* exciting and glamourous. People dressed up in their finest clothes and made a big deal about going to an airport to board a flight on a propeller-driven aircraft. Those glory days of fun and pleasant air travel are a far cry from what I have experienced.

Since the good old days of flying, lines have gotten longer; leg room has shrunk; and food has gotten, well, as you probably know, not very good. Probably the biggest difference between then and now is how a passenger behaves on an airline flight. You might say that what passengers do on a flight is questionable at best and far from glamourous.

For the most part, my airline flights are pretty smooth, and I have learned how to efficiently navigate airports and the boarding and deplaning process. I can't say that is the case with many passengers on my flights.

I learned the hard way not to sit on an aisle. I prefer to sit in a window seat, even on long flights. Aisle seats are painful when oblivious passengers wearing huge backpacks twist down the center aisle to make their way to seats at the back of the plane. I have witnessed hundreds of passengers take their aisle seats early in the boarding process and settle into their seats only to get hit in the head by a backpack. It's almost comical to watch the person wearing the backpack swing around to see what he or she hit, only to hit the passenger in the opposite aisle seat. I have been the passenger in the opposite aisle seat who took a backpack to the face.

In addition to the dangers of sitting in an aisle seat during the boarding process is the danger of taking a refreshment cart into a knee or elbow, especially if you've dozed off during a flight after a long day of travel and don't know the cart is coming. Flight attendants are on a mission to serve refreshments, and they can't always see over the service cart, so passengers beware when the cart makes its way to your row if you are sitting in the aisle seat, especially if you have your shoes off. I'll take a window seat as cheap insurance against cart injuries and other things that go up and down the center aisle of an airliner, such as people walking to the bathroom and the occasional service dog that decides to run up and down the plane. On a flight to Houston, Texas, I witnessed George, an alleged service dog that wore no vest and clearly was not trained, take a massive dump while the young headphone-wearing guy who'd brought the dog on the plane simply watch the event unfold. He didn't even budge and went back to looking at his cell phone after the dog was done, making no effort to clean up the mess. I guess he assumed the flight attendants would take care of the situation, which they didn't. Instead, the guy sitting in the same row as the dog yelled at the owner, handed him a sick bag, and forced him to clean up the pile. The smell reeked throughout the cabin all the way to Houston.

Luckily, I've only had to smell dog poop on a plane that one time in all my flying, but what's just as bad, and many times worse, is the smell of a fart on an early-morning flight. My God, what do people eat that creates gas that can melt the plastic off the ceiling of a plane? More than once, I have been in a confined seat directly behind a huge guy who must have eaten a whole cow the night before, plus cabbage, beans, and who knows what else, to cause a silent, deadly fart worse than any mustard gas attack. I can only imagine what flight attendants have to smell day after day.

Possibly the grossest and worst-smelling thing I have ever witnessed on a flight was when a clearly drunk passenger in the seat behind me took off his shoes and socks and propped up his gangrenous, stinky foot between the seats in front of him, next to my head. I turned around, carefully avoiding his nasty foot, and told him to put his foot on the floor. He was so wasted that he laughed at me while taking his foot out from between my seat and the empty one next to me, but just ten minutes later, he did it again. This time, I rang the call button and alerted the flight attendant to the situation. I thought she was going to throw up when she saw the nasty foot. She told the passenger to keep his feet on the floor, and he complied, but his foot stank just as badly when he slid it under my seat.

Ten minutes later, the fungi-covered yellow foot was next to my head again. This time, the flight attendant saw him disregard her direction, and she promptly came back to tell the guy to remove his foot and give his boarding pass to her. She looked at his boarding pass and gave him a menacing scowl.

"Sir, you are not even supposed to be in this row!" she said. "You are twenty rows back, so get your things and move immediately."

The guy laughed as he gathered his socks and shoes, got up, and walked to the back of the plane. I could see other passengers reach to cover their mouths from the smell as he passed row by row to get to the back of the plane. Once he was in his seat, the flight attendant made him put his shoes back on for the benefit of the passengers around him—or maybe to contain the biohazard.

People really need to keep their shoes and socks on when flying on an airliner but especially when they walk to the bathroom.

A guy who sat next to me on a flight to Florida removed his shoes and socks twenty minutes after takeoff. He proceeded to take out a toenail clipper and began clipping so hard that his toenails went flying all over the place. That was nasty—but not as nasty as when he pulled his right foot up to his mouth and began biting the toenail on his big toe. He worked on that thing for a good five minutes while passengers around him, including me, looked on in disbelief and took cover from any flying shrapnel. The guy later walked barefoot to the bathroom, came back to his seat after a short visit, and then began gnawing on his toe again. Let that thought sink in.

Unfortunately, that memory pops up every time I fly, especially when a meal is served, because the Toe Incident, as it has come to be known, happened right before a food service on the flight. I passed on the in-flight meal that day and instead tried to focus on the entertainment monitor in the seat back in front of me. That seemed to help distract me from the bare feet of the guy sitting next to me as he handled a sandwich with the same hands he recently had been rubbing his feet with. But the distraction of the entertainment monitor was doused when the large Samoan man in front of me flipped his huge mop of hair over his seat, entirely covering my monitor. I helplessly looked around for a flight attendant to save me from the situation. Fortunately, an elderly woman sitting next to the Samoan man noticed the hair flip and hit him in his right arm. She told him where his hair was, pointed to his headrest, and asked him to remove it. He complied but gave me a look as if he were going to kick my ass when we got off the flight and then proceeded to recline his seat as far back as possible. I was trapped and then gassed by the Samoan for the rest of the flight.

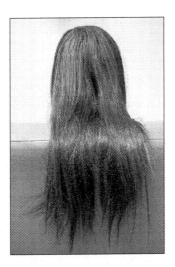

That was one of those days when I thought things couldn't get worse. They did.

On the descent into Florida, Mr. Toe, who was sitting next to me, started complaining that his stomach hurt. "That turkey sandwich must have been bad," he said.

We were twenty minutes from landing, when the big blow happened, right in between the seats of the Samoan and the old lady next to him. Plenty of puke made it onto my leg too. The good news was that I was off the hook with the Samoan, as he quickly moved his seat upright in an effort to avert another blow and then gave the kick-ass look to the guy next to me. Fortunately, it was a one-heave puke, and the flight attendants went into quick action to help clean up the mess just prior to landing. We deplaned in Florida, and I, along with the Samoan and Mr. Toe, made a stop in the men's restroom to wipe off puke from a turkey sandwich and what looked like toenails.

On my way out of the restroom, the Samoan guy looked at me while he ran a paper towel through his hair and said, "I thought flying was supposed to be fun."

I laughed and said to him, "Yeah, back in the thirties."

He didn't laugh back and gave me a look of kicking my ass again.

I hightailed it out of the restroom and made it to a rental car counter, where the line of customers was thirty-five deep. Customers were complaining about how long they had been waiting, and I noticed a young couple sitting on the floor with their shoes off, rubbing each other's feet and sharing a bag of potato chips. They alternated pulling out a chip and feeding it to each other with the hand that had just been rubbing a foot that had stepped on who knows what earlier. It was gross but not as gross as what I had witnessed on my flight that day.

That flight was certainly not glamorous and was one of many flights that made me wish it was the 1930s again.

CHAPTER 2

JITTERBUG

I hadn't heard the term *silly season* in years. My United flight to Portland, Oregon, was about to board in Denver, and the guy standing behind me in the group-two lineup continued talking to a guy in the group-one line. I thought they might be friends by the way they were chatting. "Are those Oakleys?" the guy behind me asked, pointing to a pair of white frames on the face of his new friend.

"Nah, just something I picked up when silly season started," the other man replied.

My thoughts faded to the reason I was in line to board a flight on December 27. Silly season, for me and my day job, starts around mid-November and builds all the way to the end of each calendar year. Folks needing a tax write-off or other year-end aircraft appraisals notoriously wait until the holiday season, a.k.a. the silly season, to contact me in panic mode to schedule appraisal inspections. It is a tough time of year for me, but years ago, I learned the hard way not to take my foot off the gas (jobs) when they come around.

That December 27 was one of those trips, to inspect a rare Consolidated Vultee PBY seaplane that had World War II battle history.

"Are those Johnston and Murphys?" said the guy behind me. I thought he was talking to me, but he was continuing his conversation with his neighbor.

"Group one is now boarding," an overhead speaker blasted.

The guy with the white glasses said, "See you on the plane," as his line began moving toward the jet ramp door.

"Man, those are nice shoes," muttered the guy behind me as the loudspeaker announced that group two was ready for boarding. Our line moved to the door, and folks robotically placed their cell phones on the check-in box where the gate attendant stood to make sure each passenger's phone placement made the beeping sound of approval and turned a light on the machine from red to green.

When it was my turn, I placed my old-school printed boarding pass on the machine. It didn't make a noise of approval. The light stayed red. I tried placing my ticket on the machine again, but there was no sound of approval or green light to board.

"You're good. Just go," said the attendant. "Nice shoes," she added as I put my printed ticket in my jacket pocket and headed through the door opening. Maybe the guy had been talking to me earlier.

After boarding the plane, I quickly took my seat in row ten and settled in for the quick two-hour flight to Portland. As a pilot, I always try to take seat A on the left side of a plane so I have a good idea of what the pilot sees on a flight. It's kind of a superstition of mine, but so is not sitting in a row next to a jet engine cowling, just in case an engine decides to come apart in the air. It happens.

I put in my headphones, plugged them into my phone, and hit Play on my playlist, as I do every flight, but before any music started to play, a young lady tapped my arm and asked if I was in row ten. "Yeah, it is," I replied as I looked up and noticed I was actually in row eleven. I was sure

I'd counted the rows starting at row seven, and I started visually counting the rows again from the front partition. *Seven. Eight. Ten. Eleven.*

"Wait. No row nine," I said to the lady. "Guess I am not in the right row." I gathered my stuff and unbuckled my seat belt.

"I'm sitting next to you," said the lady. "Couldn't get a seat by my husband." She pointed to a guy in the middle seat of row eight. There was an empty seat on the aisle next to him.

I settled into seat 10A and clicked the seat belt in unison with a cough from an elderly gentleman who sat in the seat ahead of me, 8A. He continued to cough as he wadded up a jacket and shoved it in between his seat and the window. He laid his head back through the opening between the seat and the window, barely touching his jacket, and coughed as he tried to go to sleep. Clearly, he was ill. *That's all I need is to get sick,* I thought to myself, as I still had several inspection trips to do before the end of the year.

"Hey, honey," said the gal in 10C to her husband in 8E, "maybe you can move to the middle seat here."

"Maybe you can switch with whoever sits in 8D when they get on," I told her.

"Thanks for that idea! I'll try that," she replied.

The elderly guy coughed in what seemed an approval of the idea.

Passengers continued to board the flight—mostly families heading home from spending Christmas with other family and friends, I imagined. One by one, passengers walked by row ten, and the seat between me and the lady in 10C remained unoccupied. *Maybe I'll get lucky and have an open seat between me and 10C today,* I thought to myself. "Come on open-seat lottery," I said under my breath.

The time for final boarding arrived, and I thought I heard the door close, but the sound was actually the old guy coughing again. *Please don't get sick. Please don't get sick,* I thought to myself.

Suddenly, a new flood of passengers began to board the plane. I thought for sure the open seat was about to be filled and probably by someone who had the flu. A guy took a seat in 8D, next to the lady's husband. "Ask that guy if he will swap seats," I told her. "Now's your chance."

"Excuse me, but would you swap seats so I can sit next to my husband?"

the young lady said to the middle-aged guy who had just sat down in seat 8D.

"Sure," he replied as the aircraft door was shut and an announcement was made to confirm that we were about to head to Portland.

"Great idea!" the lady said to me as she gathered her items and stood up to change seats. Her husband was clearly happy they could sit next to each other as she settled into her new seat.

The seat between me and my new neighbor remained empty. I had won the open-seat lottery!

My new neighbor took his seat and immediately put in some iPhone earbuds. He put a backpack under the seat in front of him but not before he took out a stack of six small leather-bound journals that looked well used. He put the stack of journals on the empty seat between us as the safety briefing announcement began on the overhead speakers. He put down his seat tray and began scribbling and drawing in one of the journals as his legs violently shook, as if he were overly nervous.

He continued to draw and write in the journal as a flight attendant walked by for a final check before takeoff. "Sir, you need to put that up," she told my neighbor. He pushed up the tray table, latched it in place, and then began shaking his legs again.

What the hell? I thought to myself as I looked at the skinny, bearded guy. He had on a Seattle Seahawks ski cap, jeans, and a red T-shirt with an outline of the state of Oregon and the word *Portland* in the middle of the outline. He looked like a typical Pacific Northwest guy, maybe heading home from a holiday gathering. He picked up another one of his journals and started to violently draw in it, pushing the tip of his pen so hard it almost went through the paper. It looked like he was drawing a pentagram. When he noticed I was looking his way, he slammed the journal closed.

The plane taxied out to the runway and lined up for takeoff, holding on the runway until it was cleared to depart. Power was added to the engines, and we began the takeoff roll.

My neighbor closed his eyes, facing straight ahead, and then moved both of his arms out in front of his midsection and turned his hands upward into a type of prayer position. The plane roared down the runway and rotated for liftoff from the ground with ease, when my neighbor's legs once again began a violent up-and-down shake. I could see the guy sitting in the aisle seat across from our row glare at the man I now referred to in my head as Jitterbug. The glare from across the aisle did not dissuade Jitterbug from continuing his leg shaking.

The plane continued a smooth climb until leveling out at a cruising altitude, when the captain came on the overhead and announced that he was turning off the seat belt sign. Immediately, Jitterbug got up out of his seat and headed to the bathroom at the rear of the plane. Coughs came from the seat in front of me as the old guy reclined his seat back, while his head was still somehow wedged between the seat and the window. Now he was even closer to me, coughing in my direction. I aimed the overhead air vent in his direction, hoping it might deflect any germs he was emitting toward me, and put on a movie on my phone.

I waited nearly twenty minutes for Jitterbug to return to his seat before I looked to the rear of the plane to see where he was. He was nowhere to be seen. *Is he still in the bathroom?* I thought to myself.

The flight attendants came by with the drink service cart and asked for my order. Then one asked, "Would your neighbor like something?"

"I don't know the guy, and he's been in the bathroom for twenty minutes," I replied.

"Okay, we'll come back," said the flight attendant.

Another fifteen minutes went by, and then the captain turned on the seat belt sign and announced that turbulence required everyone to return to his or her seat and buckle his or her seat belt. Jitterbug finally returned to his seat from his extended bathroom visit and clicked his seat belt. He pulled out a journal and once again began scribbling as hard as he could on one of the pages. His legs began to go up and down again, causing the guy in the seat in front of him to turn his head around the seat and glare at Jitterbug in disapproval. The glare didn't seem to faze Jitterbug, who went into the upward-hands prayer mode again and started a verbal meditation under his breath while his legs shook violently.

Thoughts of the shoe bomber raced through my head as Jitterbug continued verbally mediating. It didn't help that I had just watched a movie about the Charleston church shooting.

As I was about to hit the flight attendant call button, a flight attendant tapped Jitterbug on the shoulder and asked him if he needed something to drink since he had missed the drink service. He declined any refreshment, and the flight attendant gave me an awkward look, as if questioning what Jitterbug was all about. I slowly raised my shoulders and gave an expression of not knowing what was going on. The flight attendant walked to the front of the plane as Jitterbug pulled out yet another journal and began to violently draw figures in the book. I could see that the guy across the aisle was watching what Jitterbug was drawing in the journal, and he said something to the guy next to him while pointing at the journal. Jitterbug noticed that he was under observation, slammed the book closed, and put all his journals back into his backpack.

Jitterbug was doing the leg-shake again as the captain announced that we were on an initial descent into Portland and that seat backs and tray tables needed to be returned to stowed position. The elderly guy in front of me woke up to the announcement and removed his wedged head while coughing on the lady sitting next to him. She leaned away from him in visible disgust. I noticed that the two guys across the aisle had a locked-in stare with Jitterbug, apparently in case he tried to do something stupid to disrupt the flight.

A clunk from the landing gear locking in place indicated we were five miles out from landing in Portland, when I noticed Jitterbug lean down to take something out of his backpack. The two guys across the aisle leaned forward and glared at Jitterbug as if to dare him to do something stupid. Jitterbug noticed the stares, pulled his hands out of the backpack without grabbing anything, and immediately went into the hands-up position again and closed his eyes as he faced the seat ahead of him. He began the verbal meditation and didn't even notice when the pilot made one of the best greaser landings I had ever experienced. Jitterbug began shaking his legs again until he opened his eyes and noticed we were on the ground on the landing roll. His legs stopped shaking, and he leaned back in his seat in obvious relief that he was safely on the ground. He raised his arms in the air in a sign of victory that he had made it through the flight.

The two guys across the aisle looked at each other and shook their heads in disbelief that Jitterbug was just an extremely nervous flier and nothing more. They had seemed ready to roll in case there was another motive for the unusual activity.

You can never be too cautious in today's world, and if a person or situation looks questionable, say something. In that case, I was next to an incredibly nervous flier, worse than any I have seen in my million miles of flying. Unfortunately, I was also next to an incredibly sick old guy on my flight to Portland.

Forty-Eight Hours Later

I was awakened from a deep sleep by my wife coughing violently. "I don't have time to be sick!" she said as she crawled out of bed toward the bathroom. "I haven't been around anybody who's been sick either!" she added. "Or have I, Gordon?"

I thought to myself, *Ah, another bonus from the adventures of travel and a gift from the silly season.*

CHAPTER 3

BLACKOUT

Never in my life had I ever considered buying, let alone wearing, a set of insulated full-body Carhartt ranch gear to stay warm. I appreciate those who work outside in the winter months and have to bundle up to make it through the workday. I am fortunate to work in a heated office, and on frigid days, I am rarely outside long enough to worry about frostbite. But working outside on a movie set in the record-cold months of October and November in Boulder, Colorado, had me seriously thinking about buying some bulky but beautifully warm Carhartts. Twenty days of filming in the cold, both outdoors and inside a barn with a green screen and no heat, made me think about how thankful I would be to get an aircraft appraisal job in Florida, Arizona, Texas, or anywhere warm. My wish came true right after the movie wrapped, when a call came in requesting my assistance to appraise a Grumman OV-1 Mohawk in the Sunshine State of Florida. Hallelujah!

Two weeks later, I was sitting on a direct flight from Denver to Fort Lauderdale, Florida. It was an evening flight in a Boeing 737 that would depart at five o'clock from Denver and arrive after eleven o'clock Florida time. After making it through the boarding process, I took my window seat, 11F, for the nearly four-hour flight. I was eager to put my headphones in and resume a movie I had started watching on a flight a few days earlier: *Once Upon a Time in Hollywood*. It was a movie I knew my wife wouldn't enjoy; however, I was intrigued by the story and where I was in the plot as I resumed where I had previously left off. The boarding of the flight continued as I watched Brad Pitt deal with some hippies in the film, and somehow, I won the open-seat lottery for the flight. Seat 11E was vacant, and my neighbor in 11D had put on headphones and was nearly asleep as the door of the plane was closed.

We taxied out from the gate to runway eight at Denver International and made a smooth takeoff to the east. We were on our way to the Sunshine State!

As the flight leveled out, the overhead lights were turned off, and I needed to turn down the glow of my phone screen. I adjusted the brightness of my phone and continued to watch my movie as the drink cart began to make its way from the front of the cabin toward row eleven. Brad Pitt had just smoked a drug-laced cigarette in the movie, and he was tripping out as several members of Charles Manson's followers broke into his house. I thought to myself, *This is about to get real good*, as Pitt motioned to his dog to hold back.

Suddenly, my neighbor in 11D grabbed my arm, scaring the crap out of me. I pulled out my left earbud while my neighbor squeezed my arm tighter and tighter. "You okay, man?" I asked.

The guy looked at me with a glazed-over look and said, "I think I am going to black out."

"What?" I replied.

"Yeah, black out," he said, and he passed out, almost hitting his head on the seat in front of his.

I grabbed his arm with my left hand and tried shaking him as I said, "Hey! Hey!" I tried to reach for the call button above my seat but couldn't reach it as I continued to watch my neighbor, who was out cold and breathing hard. I thought he might have been having a seizure, but it did not look like seizures I had witnessed in the past.

I started waving my right arm in the air, trying to get the attention of the flight attendant serving drinks five aisles ahead of ours. She did not see me, as she was deep into her mission to serve refreshments.

With my neighbor still unconscious, I frantically thought about what to do. Thoughts of a trip I had been on from Nashville to Denver ten years before flashed in my mind. That trip hadn't turned out well for a passenger who had passed out in the back of the plane on a night flight. The situation had been eerily similar to what I was experiencing on this flight to Florida. The Nashville flight had been diverted and landed in Springfield, Missouri, my hometown as a child. The passenger who had passed out never woke up and died that night. I had watched a dead body be removed in Springfield, and I was starting to wonder if I was to witness such an event again.

Those thoughts diminished as I heard a moan from my neighbor. He slowly came back to consciousness as he arched back into his seat. "Man, you okay?" I asked.

"I don't know what is going on," he replied.

"Have you ever had that happen?" I said.

"Never. I just ... I just, like ... I think I'm going to black out—"

He keeled over again.

The flight attendant had only made it through one more row of serving drinks. I began waving my arm again and finally yelled out loud, "Hey!" That got her attention, and I pointed out my slumped-over neighbor, saying, "We have a medical here!"

The flight attendant unlocked the drink service cart and pushed it forward past row eleven so she could see what was going on.

"This guy has passed out twice, and I think we need medical attention," I said.

The flight attendant pressed the call button over my neighbor's seat to get the attention of the purser at the front of the plane. My neighbor in 11D was still out cold but breathing.

The purser walked down the aisle to our row and asked the flight attendant what was going on. The flight attendant said, "I don't know yet, but this guy is passed out. Can you make the announcement?"

The purser nodded and turned to walk back to the front of the plane.

I explained to the flight attendant that my neighbor had blacked out twice and needed medical attention. She asked if we were flying together and if we had been drinking. I replied that I had never met him before and had been watching a movie when he had the first blackout.

An overhead-announcement tone interrupted the conversation. "If there is a doctor on board, could you please ring your call button?" said the purser. There was no immediate response.

Passengers in the seats around me started looking at each other and then around the plane to see if anyone would press a call button. Nothing happened.

Another announcement was made. "If there is anyone with medical experience on board, please ring your call button." Again, there was no immediate response.

Finally, a call button was pressed, and the purser approached someone at the front of the plane.

The flight attendant continued to ask me who the guy was and what had happened as we waited for medical personnel. Just then, my neighbor in 11D came to and pulled himself back into his seat. "Sir?" said the flight attendant to my neighbor. "Are you okay?"

"Man, that has never happened to me," he said.

"Have you been drinking?" asked the flight attendant.

"A little, but I have been skiing in Utah the last four days and wonder if …" He began to fade out again but didn't completely black out this time.

"Can you grab him some water?" I asked while I noticed the purser leading a lady with blonde hair and a distinctive yellow sweater toward our row of seats.

The flight attendant poured out three waters and placed them on the fold-down table in front of the empty seat, 11E. My neighbor slammed down a cup of water as the purser introduced the medical professional. I was relieved that a qualified professional was on board, someone who might help save a guy's life and avoid another diversion like the one I had experienced in Springfield.

"Hello. I'm Divine, and I'm from Portland," said the lady in the yellow sweater. "I'm here to help."

The flight attendant told Divine that a medical kit was on the way.

"I'll get started way before it arrives," replied Divine.

The flight attendant and I looked at each other with concern at the way Divine began to engage with my neighbor.

"I can feel that you are confused," Divine said to my neighbor. He indeed looked confused but was showing signs of feeling better as he downed cups number two and three of water. The flight attendant reached over my neighbor and refilled the small cups with more water using a one-liter service bottle.

Meanwhile, Divine put her right hand behind the neck of my neighbor as she closed her eyes and slowly looked to the ceiling of the plane. She placed her left hand on the lower left arm of my neighbor and said she could feel things getting better for him. My neighbor grabbed his fourth cup of water and chugged it down.

"You want some pretzels?" the flight attendant asked him.

"I'll take two if that's okay," he replied.

The flight attendant reached over Divine and handed my neighbor two small packets of airline pretzels. He took the pretzels with his right hand, which was free. He placed one of the packets on the folding table and held on to the other packet in his right hand. He tore it open using his teeth and spit out a piece of the plastic packaging, which landed on my left arm. He noticed that he had spit on me, shrugged, and proceeded to pour the entire contents into his mouth as Divine kept her hands on him with her eyes closed toward the sky.

"Hey, I'm starting to feel better," said my neighbor just as the purser walked up with a medical kit in her hands. Divine did not move; she kept her face pointed toward the ceiling with her eyes closed, not making any sounds.

The purser placed the medical kit on the floor and returned to the front of the plane. Divine did not open the kit and continued her trancelike activity. The other passengers in the area had started to watch the event unfolding with curiosity.

My neighbor downed yet another cup of water, tore open the other packet of pretzels, and again devoured them in one pour of the packet into his mouth.

Divine opened her eyes and said, "Energy has been channeled for healing. You should be okay now." She removed her hand from behind my neighbor's neck and stood up.

"Hey, I do feel better. Thank you, Divine," he said.

The other passengers in the area began to talk among themselves as Divine removed her hand from my neighbor's forearm. "You still might want to see a doctor when you get to Florida," said Divine.

"I thought you are a doctor," said my neighbor.

"Oh, I'm a spiritual healer. Stop by and see me if you ever get to Portland," she replied, and she turned around, stepped over the medical kit, and walked back to her seat near the front of the plane.

I could see the other passengers in the area shake their heads in disbelief and then return to reading magazines, looking at their phones, and watching movies.

"Man, that lady was amazing. I feel way better now," said my neighbor as he put his headphones back on and looked at his cell phone.

I put my earbuds back in and was about to return to the climactic ending of my movie, when my neighbor grabbed my arm again. I pulled out the left earbud and turned to him. I was fully prepared for him to tell me he was about to black out again, but instead, he pulled off his headphones and reached his hand out to shake mine.

"Just want to thank you for all your help, man," he said. By then, he looked as if nothing had ever happened. "I think I was just really dehydrated from being at altitude and skiing hard the last few days," he added as he held my hand for an awkwardly long time.

"Well, if blacking out hasn't ever happened before, I strongly suggest going to see a doctor just in case," I said just as the seat belt light came on. The captain announced the upcoming descent into Fort Lauderdale, and my neighbor finally let go of my hand.

"I absolutely plan to go see a doctor," he said as he put his headphones back on and went back to looking at his phone screen.

We began the descent as I put my earbud back in and watched Leonardo DiCaprio torch a psycho lady in a swimming pool with a flamethrower. I thought to myself, *That's one of the craziest things I have ever seen*—not the flamethrower in the movie but the spiritual healer who had done her thing to help out my neighbor in seat 11D.

Twelve Hours Later

I was enjoying a sunny eighty-degree day, standing in front of a Vietnam-era turboprop plane on the ramp of a South Florida airport. It was snowing back in Denver, and there was supposed to be a high temperature of twelve degrees that day in Colorado.

As I stood in front of the OV-1 Mohawk, I thought about how nice it was that I didn't have to buy a set of Carhartts that winter.

The sun felt nice on my skin that morning. I lifted up my right hand and rotated it slowly, looking at both sides. For some reason, I had a sense of renewed energy that day.

CHAPTER 4

Zero Tolerance

A nearly twenty-year adventure began in the downtown Denver office of XCell Cellular in 1998. Our company was formed to buy and build cellular telephone service areas, and the Denver office was the headquarters to backhaul billing information and house our technical and sales staff.

One spring day, while I sat in the office, making sales calls, the door squealed, and our sales manager, Bob, came bounding in with a big smile on his face. "Let me take you back to your childhood," he said as he tossed me a wrapped candy.

It had been one of my favorites as a kid: a root beer barrel.

"This will make your day," Bob said.

I took a deserved break from my cold-calling, unwrapped the candy, and tossed it into my mouth, awaiting a burst of flavor I had experienced many times as a child. I bit down to release the liquid center. *Crack!*

The sound wasn't the candy breaking; it was my molar breaking. It was a sound I had never heard and an experience I had never felt, and it left me silent in shock.

"Like nothing you've ever had," said Bob.

"You could say that," I replied as I spit out the candy and half a tooth.

Bob looked at my hand and said, "Well, that sucks." He pulled some more candy out of the bag, tossed another my way, and then walked into the other room to offer some to the rest of the staff.

I thought about leaving the office and driving to a dental office, but I felt no pain. I ran my tongue over the void in my tooth and decided to wait to see a dentist about the break until my normal teeth cleaning, which was in a couple of weeks. Back to work I went, but the extra unwrapped candy went into the trash.

Two weeks later, at my dental appointment, my dentist inspected the broken tooth and told me that as long as it didn't hurt, there was no need to do anything.

"You will know when to come see me," he declared at the end of the appointment. He also announced that he was retiring in a few months.

Months went by, and I received a letter in the mail that my old dentist had retired, and the office was closing. My broken tooth hadn't bothered me, and instead of seeking a new dentist, I put off going to another dentist for any cleanings or other dental issues. That was a bad idea.

Five Years Later

Like a lot of other folks, I frequent Starbucks in the morning for a cup of Pike's Place black coffee to get me going each day. It's a wonderful treat that I look forward to, but little did I know what my morning cup of coffee was about to do to me that day in Lafayette, Colorado.

I waited my turn in line until the barista who served me morning after morning handed me a steaming cup of hot coffee. I was a regular, and she knew my drink.

"Have a nice day," said the barista as I gently took my first sip.

"What the hell?" I screamed.

Something was wrong—not with the coffee but with the tooth next to my broken molar. A sharp pain hit the nerve of the tooth and almost sent me to my knees. The barista looked at me in horror and asked if the coffee was okay.

"Yeah, just a weird pain in a tooth that has never bothered me," I said.

Another rush of nerve pain hit me like nothing I had ever experienced. It felt like an electrical shock that went through my tooth, up the nerve, and straight to my head.

"Oh my God!" I said out loud. I felt as if I were about to pass out.

"You need to go next door and have that looked at," said the barista.

A franchised dental office had recently moved in next to the Starbucks. I didn't know anything about it, but I decided I had to visit it right away.

I handed the coffee back to the barista and almost dropped it as another wave of pain pierced my tooth. I was sure it was the molar next to the broken tooth after I ran my tongue over the broken void, which didn't generate any pain.

I made my way to the dental office next door and begged to see a dentist to look at my situation. Thankfully, I was in a dental chair just thirty minutes later.

An older gentleman entered the room and introduced himself as the dentist who would be helping me. I explained that the tooth next to my broken molar was generating excruciating pain and that I needed help.

"We're going to do a cold test," said the dentist as his assistant looked on.

The assistant then left to get supplies to do the test. She came back with a tray of supplies, and the dentist asked me to open up so he could apply the test. He applied a cold nugget of nitrogen to the molar I thought was the source of pain that morning. Nothing happened.

"We're going to apply this to that broken molar now," he said.

"That one's okay," I insisted.

Was I ever wrong!

He applied the cold test, sending me into the worst pain I have ever felt in my life. I nearly shot out of the chair. The dentist looked at the assistant and told her to clear his morning appointments.

"You need a root canal on that broken tooth," said the dentist. "I can do that this morning," he added.

"How could that be?" I asked myself. Then the memory of my former dentist's words hit: "You will know when to come see me." Little did I know what I would endure over the next four hours in the dental chair.

Ten Years Later

The broken molar never really felt right after I had the root canal done, even with the crown that had filled the void where the root beer barrel candy had done its damage.

I had gone back for cleanings to the dentist in Lafayette, but my wife and daughter had recently started working with a dental office in Boulder, Colorado, and convinced me to start going there to get a family discount.

The first cleaning, complete with x-rays, revealed a problem with the broken molar. The crown wasn't seated properly, but worse was an infection discovered in my gums in the same area of the molar. The hygienist called in the owner of the dental office and showed her my x-rays. After a brief review of the film, the dentist told me I had to immediately go to an endodontist. There was a major problem that needed to be fixed right away. Their office set up an appointment for me the next day, despite my efforts to delay any other dental appointments, as I had a trip to Seattle scheduled to film a pilot for an upcoming TV show in Canada.

We had spent months planning the filming, and a crew was driving from Vancouver, Canada, to Everett, Washington, with film gear to meet with me and the host of the series. We were to film an episode centered on a World War II Mitsubishi Zero fighter aircraft I was involved with. The filming date could not be changed, as we had to meet a production deadline.

Despite my desire to delay another dental appointment, I went to the endodontist the next day to have my tooth looked at, and the news was worse than I could have imagined.

I found out why there was such immediacy for me to see an endodontist. He took new x-rays and announced that he hoped I had blocked out the morning so he could do another root canal. I was in dental hell again for the rest of the morning, and as a bonus, the endodontist discovered that one of the roots had been missed on the first go-around.

All was looking good, the fillings were about to go in, and I was assured the procedure was near completion. It looked as if I could make my flight the next day in better shape than when I had arrived that morning. That was, until the endodontist asked his assistant to bring in a microscope to look at something strange.

The endodontist placed a microscope in my mouth and said, "That's what I thought."

I have learned in life that "That's what I thought" is never a good phrase, and I was right. The endodontist discovered that the root beer barrel candy had done way more damage than breaking the outside of my molar off; it had cracked the tooth vertically.

"It has to be extracted," said the endodontist. "We can't do any more here. I'll put in a temporary filling that should last a few days, but it needs to come out soon."

I told the doctor about my trip the next day to Everett and how important it was that I be there.

"Is it okay for me to fly tomorrow for work?" I asked.

"The temporary filling should be okay if you don't eat on that side of your mouth," he replied. "You must have a high pain tolerance to have gone this long," he added. "But get that thing out the minute you are back home."

He turned to his assistant and told her to get me scheduled for a procedure. The endodontist finished putting in the temporary filling, and I left his office that day thinking about the upcoming tooth pulling but happy I would be able to make the filming the next day.

Twelve Hours Later

I was in seat 11A from Denver to Seattle, and we were smoothly climbing to a cruising altitude of thirty-six thousand feet. The two-hour-and-forty-minute flight would put me on the ground in Seattle with two hours to spare to fight the I-5 traffic north to Paine Field in Everett. I was thinking about what I was going to say on film that afternoon, when *wham!* The shock of tooth pain resonated through my entire body as the molar that had just been worked on began to throb. The airliner continued to climb until leveling out at cruising altitude. I thought about the time remaining on the flight and what I would do if I made it to Seattle.

Will I need to get an extraction up there? I thought to myself as the pain suddenly went away. *Maybe I will be okay and just take care of it in Denver.*

Wham. Another wave of pain came. Then the shock went away again.

That went on for another two-plus hours until we landed in Seattle.

What should I do? I wondered as we deplaned.

My cell phone buzzed, announcing receipt of a message: "Made it through the border and almost in Everett with the film crew. See you soon." It was from the director for the filming that day.

I didn't want to let everyone down, so I got a rental car, drove to a nearby Walgreens, and bought three tubes of Orajel. The gel had helped my kids when they were teething as infants, so I thought it might help my situation of on-again, off-again pain.

I used an entire tube of Orajel on the forty-five-minute drive to Paine Field. It barely took the edge off my tooth pain, but it was better than nothing.

I arrived at Legend Flyers in Everett, where a Japanese Zero was under restoration, just as the film crew was unloading a van full of gear.

"We have to make this shoot quick so we can get back and cross the border today," said the director. "You okay?" she added.

"Just a little pain," I replied, trying to ignore my tooth.

"Let's try to get everything in one take," said the director as the film crew set up lights and cameras in the hangar by the Zero.

I was in excruciating pain and spread another tube of Orajel on my gums just as the director told me and the host of the show to take our places.

"And action!" said the director.

The host asked me about a gun site on display next to the Japanese fighter plane. I began to describe the gun site to the host, when *wham!* Another shock of pain hit me. I ignored the pain and continued to point at the World War II artifact and describe why it was rare.

"And cut!" said the director. "Wow, you looked really serious, Gordon. Great job!" she said as the crew reset for the next shot.

I somehow finished the day of filming, mostly thanks to the third tube of pain medication I applied during a break in the action. The film crew got what they needed for the TV show, and I made it back to Denver, enduring the same tooth pain I'd had on the flight up to Seattle. It was a horrible experience I wouldn't wish on anyone.

Two days later, the tooth that had given me years of pain was extracted, and I began a one-year process for an implant to replace the void. I wasn't in any tooth pain for the first time in years—pain that had been caused by a single root beer barrel candy and exacerbated on a flight, all in the name of aviation history.

A great adventure is always painful in one way or another.

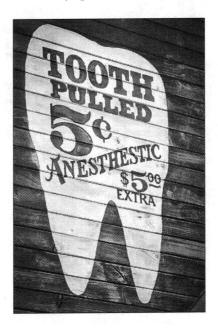

CHAPTER 5

UPGRADE TO FIRST

Mardi Gras, or Fat Tuesday, is one of my favorite celebrations of the year. I love the tradition, the drinks, and the food, especially a good king cake complete with a plastic baby Jesus baked in for good luck. How I wished I were flying to New Orleans on a cold winter day in Denver, but instead, I was flying from Denver to Portland and then driving two and a half hours one way to look at a World War II German fighter plane for a client. It wasn't Mardi Gras, but I was celebrating the fact that I was going to see one of my favorite World War II fighters and would have a chance to crawl all around it.

I was running behind and missed grabbing a coffee or any breakfast that morning. I was reminded of that fact when my stomach growled angrily on the train to terminal B at Denver International Airport. Just as

I arrived at the gate to board the flight to Portland, the gate agent made an overhead announcement.

"Mr. Page, if you are in the boarding area, please see me here at the front desk," said the agent.

I walked to the desk and announced myself to the female gate agent.

"It's your lucky day," she said. She handed me a new boarding pass that replaced my original seat assignment of 9A. "You're in first today. Have a nice flight."

My stomach growled again as I took my boarding pass and went to the group-one boarding line.

I had been upgraded to seat 4A, which meant I should get something to drink once I was in my seat, and even better, a real breakfast would be served instead of a bag of pretzels. Mardi Gras was shaping up nicely.

Proceeding down the Jetway, I boarded the Boeing 737 and immediately noticed that *Star Wars* music was playing overhead. It was a familiar Darth Vader theme song, "The Imperial March." I thought it was odd that music was playing, until I noticed a large brass plaque alerting passengers that the aircraft was a limited-edition *Star Wars*–painted aircraft to commemorate the movie *The Rise of Skywalker*. I had seen some photos of the plane on different websites and couldn't believe my luck that I was on board such a special-edition plane. I asked the flight attendant who was greeting the boarding passengers if it was indeed the *Star Wars* plane. She confirmed it was. "You wouldn't know it because passengers walk down the Jetway, board the plane, and never see it from the outside," she said.

"Are there Storm Troopers for flight attendants?" I asked.

"Uh, no. And you aren't the first to ask that question," she replied while rolling her eyes. She motioned for me to keep moving down the aisle.

I took my seat, and it wasn't long before a guy sat next to me and asked how my day was going. He had just gotten back from a family trip to Costa Rica the night before and said he was doing a day trip to Portland to look at a construction project.

"You doing anything fun today?" he asked as he clicked his seat belt.

"Yeah, looking at planes but not as cool as the one we are on," I replied.

He looked at me with confusion. "Why is this plane cool? I fly these all the time."

"It's the *Star Wars* plane!" I said with excitement.

"Uh, okay," he responded just as a flight attendant walked to our row and asked if we wanted anything to drink.

"Water for me," said my neighbor.

"I need coffee," I said to the attendant. "Kinda disappointed you aren't in a Storm Trooper outfit," I added with a laugh.

The flight attendant glared at me, turned around, and fought his way upstream with passengers who were boarding the plane.

"This day is starting out great!" I said to my neighbor.

"Not for me," he replied. "Had to drive two hours after no sleep last night, so I'll be out in a bit. No coffee for me; I gotta get some rest. Besides, I can never finish a cup of hot coffee before the flight takes off."

The flight attendant returned to our row and handed a cup of water and two small paper napkins to my neighbor. "I'll be right back for you," he said to me with a revenge tone in his voice.

"Whoa, that was kind of nasty," said my neighbor.

"Maybe he is a real Storm Trooper," I replied with a weak laugh.

Passengers continued to flow onto the plane. None of them noticed they were on the *Star Wars* plane.

I could see the flight attendant fighting his way between passengers while balancing a coffee cup in his hands. He arrived at our row and gingerly handed me the fullest cup of hot coffee I had ever been served. It was filled to the brim and spilled out a bit onto my hand as I took the cup. The flight attendant turned around and fought his way through passengers back to the front of the plane.

I stayed as focused as I could to slowly pull the cup of coffee over my neighbor and toward the small area between our seats, where his water was placed. He crossed the legs of his light-colored pants in an effort to protect himself. The *Star Wars* music continued to play, and it was as if my movements were choreographed to Darth Vader's theme as the cup of hot coffee inched slowly toward me.

"Hey, Mom!" said a young boy walking down the aisle next to my neighbor. "It's *Star Wars*!" Gleefully, he turned to his right, swinging his backpack into my neighbor.

The backpack hit my neighbor right in his face, which caused him to raise his hand in self-defense. That was when the crescendo of the music and all else in life began to play in slow motion.

In reaction to what was happening, I pulled the hot cup of coffee toward me as fast as I could, and the cup decided to collapse from the death grip I had on it. Eight ounces of steaming-hot coffee poured into my lap and drenched the Levi's I had specially worn for the airplane inspection that day. I tried to stand up to stop the flow of molten liquid in my seat, but my seat belt kept me locked in place as the hot coffee made its way to the middle of the seat.

"Here! Take these," said my stunned neighbor as he handed me the two small paper napkins.

I took the napkins and frantically started soaking up the hot coffee.

Another flight attendant walked by as I was wiping and wringing out the tiny napkins as fast as I could.

My neighbor held out his hand to stop another flight attendant and asked, "Can we get some napkins here, please?"

The attendant glared at my neighbor and replied, "This isn't my area, and I don't have napkins." He proceeded to walk to the back of the plane just as the main cabin door closed.

I was soaked, and it looked as if I had a major bladder leakage problem. Hot coffee had strategically stained me in the crotch.

The flight attendant who had served me the hot coffee was making a final check of the area and picking up drink cups from passengers in the first-class cabin. He took my empty cup and said, "You must have been thirsty."

I tried to show him what had happened, motioning to my lap in the hope that he would show mercy and get me a towel or something to help with the drying process of my pants. My neighbor tried to help by asking for some napkins. The flight attendant left, returned with two more small paper napkins, and then abruptly returned to the front of the plane for takeoff. It was too little too late, but I used the small napkins, turned on the overhead vent to the highest setting, and pointed it toward my lap.

"Man, that's horrible," said my neighbor as the plane taxied out for takeoff. "What are you going to do?"

There was nothing I could do at that point other than hope the next two hours of flying would help dry my jeans to a point that wasn't as embarrassing as the initial downpour.

"Well, I guess I'm predisastered for the rest of the day," I responded.

"That's one of the greatest attitudes I have ever heard," said my neighbor. "Could have spilled on me," he added. "Must be my lucky day." He put on his headphones and fell asleep.

Thirty minutes later, the female flight attendant who had greeted me at boarding handed me a tray with a morning breakfast meal. "Would you like something to drink?" she asked.

"I think I'm good with drinks today," I replied while trying to hide my wet crotch.

The best part of the meal that morning was the large cloth napkin the silverware was wrapped in. I used it to dry my seat and pants, and it seemed to help.

I held on to the napkin even after the meal tray was picked up and used it until the final walk-through by the flight attendants prior to our landing in Portland.

The attendant who had originally given me the hot coffee came by our row, asking if we had any items for pickup. I handed him the soaked cloth napkin and told him to have a nice day. He glared at me as he gingerly took the soaked napkin and carried it like a dirty diaper to the front of the plane.

We landed safely in Portland, and the Darth Vader theme began to play again as we taxied to the arrival gate.

"Good luck on your trip," said my neighbor as we got out of our seats to deplane. "I'm gonna use that predisastered thing," he added as he grabbed his backpack and left the plane.

The two hours of air vent and the use of the cloth napkin had helped to dry my dark Levi's to a point where someone would really have had to look closely to notice they were wet. Regardless, I had to press on to make my appointment.

Three Hours Later

I drove over Mount Hood and some spectacular scenery on Highway 26 from Portland to Madras, Oregon, and safely arrived at a hangar full of World War II aircraft. In particular was a German Me 109 that I was to inspect.

Upon entering the facility, I was greeted by a receptionist who told me the mechanic I was to meet with was still at lunch.

"Can I get you a cup of coffee while you wait?" she asked. "Smells like some just got brewed," she added while pointing her nose up and sniffing the air.

"Thanks, but I'm good on coffee," I said. "I'll get started with my photos if that's okay."

She pointed me in the direction of the 109, which sat in the middle of the hangar. "Go ahead, and I will let the guys know you are here when they get back," she said.

I walked over to the Luftwaffe fighter plane and smelled my forearm as I held up my phone to begin taking photos. It was me who smelled like freshly brewed coffee, not the breakroom. I reached down to feel my pants, which were still a little wet.

But all was good. I was doing what I loved. It was Mardi Gras.

CHAPTER 6

MR. SMITH

The Antonov An-124 cargo jet is a monster of a plane. I have seen several around the world, including in Denver, Colorado, as they are leased for strategic airlifts to transport heavy cargo. I witnessed the big brother to the An-124, the An-225, fly in the Paris Air Show, and I was amazed that such a huge plane could leave the earth, even if it had six jet engines to power it.

I had a couple of hours to kill on a rainy morning in Everett, Washington, so I decided to walk across the parking lot of the hotel I was staying at near Paine Field to see what was on display at the Boeing Future of Flight building. I had been in the facility before, which is the starting point for the Boeing tour, which takes visitors to the Boeing plant to see how their jets are made. The production facility itself is massive. It is the largest building in the world by volume at 472,370,319 cubic feet and covers a whopping 98.7 acres. This is the factory where the wide-body Boeing 747, 767, 777, and 787 Dreamliner are assembled, and I see the newly built jets come and go during my stays in Everett.

I didn't have time for a Boeing tour that day and mainly wanted to see what might be on sale at the Boeing store. But as I entered the Future of Flight facility, I noticed the nose of an Antonov An-124 Ruslan filling the three-story glass wall at the back of the building.

"What is that thing doing here?" I asked as I approached the receptionist.

"Couldn't tell you," replied the elderly lady manning the desk. "For twelve dollars, you can go see for yourself. And you can go to the observation deck for a good view too."

I paid the entry fee and immediately headed to a large metal ramp that led to the lower level of the building. The nose of the An-124 was nearly pressed up against the glass wall, and it dominated any view to the ramp area it was parked on. However, I could see past the Antonov that an even bigger plane was parked behind it, near a building labeled "Dreamlifter Operations." That plane was a Boeing-built Dreamlifter, an overgrown Boeing 747 that was used to transport components for the 787 Dreamliner.

I immediately looked for a way to get to the observation deck for a better view of the two huge aircraft. I found a staircase that led to the top of the building and exited a glass door that put me on the observation deck. The view of Paine Field was spectacular from that vantage point, as was the view of the Antonov An-124 and the Boeing Dreamlifter. It was hard to get photos of the planes due to their size, but I managed to get some memories on my cell phone before I had to leave for SeaTac Airport.

A solid two hours of driving in heavy Seattle traffic got me to SeaTac Airport with no time to spare. Somehow, I got through the security check quickly, and then I dashed to gate A10 just as the gate agents were starting the boarding process.

I took my window seat, 11A, for the flight back to Denver, and a tall elderly man took the aisle seat moments after I buckled in. He had a small gray backpack that he carefully placed under the seat in front of him. The backpack looked important to him by the way he scooted it deep into the area with his hands. He gently rubbed his hand on the backpack before leaning back into his seat. He was so tall that he had to turn his knees toward the empty seat area between us, mostly to avoid other passengers who kept running into him while they boarded the plane.

As the boarding process continued, I noticed that several men of the same age as the guy in 11C patted his shoulder as they walked by. Obviously, they knew my neighbor, based on the way they greeted him. My neighbor remained quiet during the boarding process other than to acknowledge whoever walked by and patted his shoulder. I wasn't sure if I should know who my neighbor was by the way people seemed to know him, especially after ten passengers made the effort to say hello to him.

Fortunately for the tall man in 11C, the seat between us was open for the flight. He could stretch out a bit in the area of the open seat, and the space helped him keep the drink cart from hitting his knees during the flight. He remained quiet but did order two whiskeys from the drink cart when it came by.

I noticed him tip his drink toward his backpack in silence before he downed the double whiskey in one continuous gulp.

My neighbor sat in silence for the rest of the trip until we began the descent into Denver International Airport. Then he asked me, "Do you know the Denver airport well?"

"Yeah, I'm from Denver," I answered. "You going anywhere fun today?"

"Gotta catch a connection to Jackson Hole," he said.

"I love that place," I replied. "You doing some skiing?"

"Kind of," said the neighbor. "It's my wife's favorite place."

"Fantastic!" I replied. "Is she with you on this flight?"

"Yes, she is," he said as he looked at the backpack under the seat. "This will be her last trip to Jackson. A bunch of buddies are on this plane to go with us to Jackson."

"Sounds like you are going to make some good memories," I said.

My neighbor's eyes welled up with tears at my comment. He gently rubbed his right foot on the backpack.

"I'm sorry. Did I say something?" I asked.

"Ann was a great skier and my best friend. Lost her to cancer," he said while rubbing a tear away.

"Oh. So sorry for your loss," I said. "I hope you *have* good memories of her," I added.

"Thanks for that," he said as he pulled up the backpack and put it in the seat between us. He gently put his hand around the backpack and pulled it tightly to his side.

He was silent again until we landed in Denver. I didn't know what else to say until we deplaned from the flight.

"I hope you have a good trip to Jackson Hole," I said as we walked out of the Jetway. "And I'm sorry for your loss."

He teared up again and didn't say anything, but several of his buddies approached him in the gate area and put their arms out to comfort him. I noticed that several of his buddies were speaking in Russian as they hugged him and began to guide him away from the gate area. I had no idea what my neighbor was going through, but I was glad he had friends to support him on his trip to Jackson Hole.

My day had started with a Russian Antonov, and I wondered if my neighbor on the flight might have been Russian as I walked toward the moving walkway to exit the airport.

I never got my neighbor's name, just his wife's: Ann. But I was sure I had sat next to her that day.

CHAPTER 7

SEAT 29B

Savannah, Georgia, is the oldest city in the Peach State and attracts millions of visitors each year with its cobblestone streets, historic buildings, food, and pure Southern hospitality. It is full of history and charm, and part of its history is especially important to my family and me. Savannah was where our uncle Bill and thousands of other airmen trained in World War II.

In January 1942, the Mighty Eighth Air Force was established at the Savannah Army Air Base, now Hunter Army Airfield, and thousands of bomber crews were trained there to defend the United States during World War II. The history of the Mighty Eighth Air Force is on display in the western suburbs of Savannah, in Pooler, Georgia, at the National Museum of the Mighty Eighth Air Force, a fantastic facility not to be missed. Thanks to a business trip, I had an opportunity to get in a quick visit that would mean a lot to me and our uncle Bill.

I flew to Atlanta, Georgia; rented a car; and drove three and a half hours to Savannah to meet with folks at the Gulfstream factory, FlightSafety, and if all fell into place, I would make it to the Mighty Eighth Air Force museum before it closed. I hoped to see our uncle Bill's 491st Bomb Group display at the Mighty Eighth museum. He had told me there was a photo at the museum of his plane, *Tenderfoot*, about to crash on a beach in Dover, England. He had shown me a copy of the original photo a few years before and proudly pointed out the top of his head near the gunner's position of the starboard side of the plane. Moments later, it ended up as scrap on the beach. All but one of the crew survived the crash, and according to Uncle Bill, it was the sole airman who bailed out who didn't make it that day.

I arrived at the Gulfstream factory on time to have a scheduled meeting about our software product. The meeting included an amazing tour of the factory, which gave me a true appreciation for the technology and innovation that go into a Gulfstream jet, as well as the luxuries that go along with owning one.

After a quick stop by the FlightSafety Savannah Gulfstream Learning Center, I made my way to the museum with only an hour before closing to see Uncle Bill's display. After making my way past the museum rotunda, I quickly explored some amazing exhibits until I came upon the 491st Bomb Group display. There it was: Uncle Bill's head peeking above the gunner's position opening on the B-24 bomber *Tenderfoot*, which was about to crash-land.

It was a proud moment for me, one I couldn't wait to share with Uncle Bill when I was back in Denver. I took a photo of the display and then asked a museum visitor to take one of me with the display in the background to document the moment. It had been a great day, and I had another full day ahead of me to explore Savannah before heading back to Colorado.

My cell phone rang as I was admiring the bomb group display. It was Tracey, my wife, and I was excited to tell her about the photo and the rest of my day.

"Hey, hon!" I said as I answered the phone. "You won't believe what I'm looking at: Uncle Bill's bomber group and his photo."

My wife replied, "It's Uncle Bill I'm calling about."

"Awesome! I can't wait to show him my photos when I get back," I said.

"He's gone," said Tracey.

"Gone where?"

"He slipped in the tub. He's gone," Tracey replied. "Can you get back home sooner. Aunt Ruby really needs us."

I was struck with grief, not knowing what to say.

"Hon? You there?" said Tracey.

"Yeah, I'll see if I can fly standby and get back tomorrow," I replied. "I'll call you later. Gotta go."

"Hang in there, and call me later," Tracey said, and she hung up the phone.

I was stunned as I stood in front of Uncle Bill's photo. I would never get the chance to talk with him about the 491st display and how proud I was to see the top of his head in the photo of the *Tenderfoot*.

Instead of getting the pleasure of enjoying some Savannah hospitality that evening and the next day, I made the three-hour-plus drive back to Atlanta. I had booked a room at a Hilton hotel on the north side of Hartsfield-Jackson Atlanta Airport so I could catch an early flight back to Denver the next morning. I called the airline on the drive back to Atlanta to reschedule my flight. All flights the next day were oversold, but when I told the airline agent about the situation at home, I was added to the standby list for the first flight out. I would have to be at the airport by five o'clock the next morning to catch a six o'clock flight. It would be a short night of sleep, as I wouldn't be at the hotel until nine o'clock that night, and the eastern time zone difference of two hours would make it an even shorter night in my mind. My internal clock meant a two o'clock wake-up call. Don't ask; it's one of my travel quirks.

As I got closer to Atlanta, I remembered a Cajun-style restaurant near the hotel, called Spondivits. I had eaten there years before, and the idea of Cajun food was comforting, so I put the address into the GPS and headed toward what I thought might make my day a little better.

I turned off of I-85 onto Virginia Avenue toward the restaurant and was surprised to see half a dozen police cars with lights flashing in the parking lot of a Waffle House next to Spondivits. That didn't stop me from finding a parking place in the back of the restaurant and walking toward the entrance. A policeman stopped me as I was at the top of the parking lot and asked if I had seen what had happened. I responded that I had just arrived from Savannah and was going into the Cajun place for a bite to eat.

"What happened?" I asked the cop.

"Shooting. One dead," he replied.

Looking past the cop, I could see a sheet over a body on the floor by the counter at the Waffle House.

"Be careful," said the cop. He got on his radio and said, "One coming up for Spondivits."

I continued into the restaurant and sat at the bar. It wasn't long before a guy sat next to me and said that he had witnessed the shooting as he was walking into Spondivits an hour earlier. "Tough day for someone at the Waffle House," he said.

"Yeah, been a tough day," I replied, thinking about Uncle Bill.

I had a beer and a great bowl of gumbo while enjoying good conversation, until I realized it was eleven o'clock. I paid my tab, bid farewell to the guy next to me, and exited the restaurant. The police had left, the body had been removed, and it looked like business was back to normal at the Waffle House as I drove away to the nearby Hilton.

Four in the morning came just as I thought it would: quickly. I didn't sleep much that night, as I was thinking about the shooting at the Waffle House and also Uncle Bill. I got to the Atlanta airport by five o'clock, as planned, and made it to the gate at five thirty for the flight back to Denver. The boarding process was well underway, and I saw on the status board that I was first in line on the standby list. My fingers were crossed as passenger after passenger got on the flight. Things were not looking good for me, until I heard a voice on the overhead speaker: "Mr. Page, if you are in the boarding area, please see me at the front desk."

I approached the desk, and after a brief exchange with the agent, I had a boarding pass in hand. I got the last seat on the flight to Denver: 29B.

I made my way down the Jetway as fast as I could, as I could see the flight attendant on the plane holding a microphone and announcing the door was about to close. I walked by the flight attendant as she continued her announcements and made my way to row twenty-nine. There was one single open seat: 29B. On either side of the open seat were two huge southern women in matching flowered muumuu-type dresses. They both had big hair, long fingernails, and large handbags that they held in their laps.

"You in the middle seat?" said the lady on the aisle as I stuffed my bag into the last remaining space in the overhead.

"I am," I replied.

She proceeded to grab the top of the seat in front of her and pull her body out of seat 29C. The old lady in the seat she had grabbed screamed as her seat reclined. "Sorry about that, honey," said the lady who'd caused the incident. She was now standing in the aisle, waiting for me to take my middle seat.

I slid into my seat and immediately thought something was wrong. There was very little room, thanks to the lady in seat 29A. "You don't mind if I keep the armrest up, do you?" the lady in 29A asked. I then noticed that the other armrest of the lady in 29C was up also. "I can't get the armrest down all the way anyway," said the lady in 29A.

"I guess that will have to work," I said, wondering how bad I was about to be sandwiched in between the two ladies.

I found out just how bad when the lady in 29C grabbed the headrest of 28C again and held on to it to help lower herself back into her seat. The old lady screamed again as folds of fat from the ladies on both sides of me squished me into my seat.

"Boy, is it ever hot in here," said the lady in 29C to her pal. She reached up to point the overhead air vent in the direction of her sweating underarm, which fell on my shoulder when she put her arm down. I could already feel the sweat on my left shoulder from the arm of the lady in 29A.

"It's gonna be a long flight," said 29A to her twin in 29C.

I thought to myself, *God, is it ever*, as the plane pushed back for the nearly three-hour flight to Denver. I tried to ignore the situation and was just glad I was going to get home to help support my family in a time of need. At about the same time, the ladies pulled out tarot cards from their bags.

The entire flight home, I watched the ladies lay out tarot cards on the fold-down tables in front of them. I endured a lot of moaning and the words "Mmm, mmm, mmm" as the cards turned over. It was indeed a long flight home as I sat in silence, feeling the sweat that soaked the sleeves of my shirt.

Despite the squishing of my body for nearly three hours, I survived the flight from Atlanta to Denver in one piece. The muumuu twins walked ahead of me up the aisle of the plane, slowly down the Jetway, and into the gate area. As I was thinking about the drive home, the lady who had sat in the aisle next to me said, "Honey, things are going to get better."

"Thanks?" I replied.

Could the tarot cards she read have told her I lost an uncle? I wondered as I left the gate area.

"Nah," I said to myself. She knew what I had endured that morning in seat 29B.

CHAPTER 8

THREE SHEETS TO VEGAS

The National Business Aviation Association, or NBAA, is a nonprofit organization that has a mission to foster an environment that allows business aviation to thrive in the United States and around the world. With more than eleven thousand members, the NBAA collects, interprets, and disseminates operational and managerial data related to the safe, efficient, and cost-effective use of business aircraft. One of the ways the NBAA shares information is through an annual Business Aviation Convention and Exhibition. It is one of the largest trade shows in the United States, and because of the size of the show, it requires a convention center that can support the exhibits and attendees.

The NBAA alternates the convention between the Orange County

Convention Center in Orlando, Florida, and the Las Vegas Convention Center in Nevada.

My travel schedule worked out that I would get to go to the NBAA convention when it was in Las Vegas. I looked forward to seeing all the exhibits, including full-size airplanes and helicopters on display, along with hundreds of vendors, many of whom I work with and only get to see once a year.

Because the show was in Las Vegas, I could count on some long days and even longer nights in the city that doesn't sleep. Little did I know the craziness of Las Vegas would begin on an early-morning flight from Denver.

I booked my flight to Las Vegas at the last minute, and the only seats available were middle or aisle seats. The only flight available was a 7:00 a.m. departure, and begrudgingly, I picked an aisle seat. I knew I would once again be in the danger zone of backpacks and other luggage during the boarding process, but the middle seat has its own dangers: the unknown passengers on either side.

On the day of my trip to NBAA, I arrived at Denver International Airport early and made good time through security and on to the departure gate without any problems. Folks in the gate area were half-asleep, and there wasn't much activity, except for a guy who was pacing in front of the glass windows that looked out to the Boeing 737 that would take us to Las Vegas. The guy looked as if he had not slept the night before. His short blond hair was a mess, and he was wearing torn jeans, a vintage Metallica band T-shirt, and some old Converse tennis shoes. He looked as if he could have been at a concert the previous night and partied with the band.

"Woo-hoo! Vegas!" shouted the guy, causing the groggy folks in the gate area to perk up. He looked as if he needed a cigarette to calm him down. He also looked as if he'd had plenty to drink and who knew what else in preparation for the trip to Vegas. "Yeah!" he said loudly as he threw his fist in the air. "Let's get going!"

I began to chant in my head as I watched the guy continue pacing back and forth, *Please don't let me sit by him. Please don't let me sit by him.*

The gate agent announced the boarding of the flight, and folks in the gate area began to make their way to the door, including Woo-Hoo Guy.

Please don't let me sit by him, I said again to myself as Woo-Hoo Guy boarded several passengers ahead of me.

I placed my boarding pass on the check-in stand, and a flight attendant verified I was okay to board. She looked at me with a look of sorrow as I continued past her and onto the Jetway. "Good luck," she said.

That was nice, I thought. *Wishing me luck in Vegas.*

"Thanks," I replied as I continued on.

I made my way onto the plane and walked down the aisle to my seat: 11C.

There he was. Woo-Hoo Guy was in seat 11A. The attendant at the gate must have known, and that was why she'd wished me luck.

Woo-Hoo was pretending to drum on the fold-down table in front of him, which was in the down position.

"What's up, man?" he said as I placed my backpack under the seat in front of me.

"Just heading to Vegas for a show," I replied.

"Yeah! Vegas!" said the guy. "I was at a show last night."

I could tell he was telling the truth by the way he reeked of booze and cigarettes.

"What sweet show you seeing in Vegas?" he asked as he continued to beat the seat tray.

"An airplane show, man," I said.

"Cool! I haven't seen them in concert," he replied as he went back to drumming. He pulled a plastic water bottle out of the seat pocket in front of him, took off the top, and then took a big swig. It smelled like vodka as he wiped off his mouth, put the lid back on the bottle, and put it back in the webbing of the seat back.

A flight attendant walked by, and the guy waved his hand at her. "Can I get a beer?" he said.

"We will have a drink service after takeoff, sir," she responded.

"Bummer," he replied as he took the water bottle out and took another swig.

It definitely smelled like booze.

The boarding process continued, and I felt bad for whoever was going to have to sit in the middle seat next to Woo-Hoo Guy. But the seat remained empty as the main cabin door closed.

"Yeah! More room!" the guy said as he put down the tray table in front of the empty seat.

A flight attendant making the final check before takeoff came by, looked at me, and told me I had to put the tray table up. I complied, and the attendant told the guy in 11A to put his up too.

"Hey, can I get a beer?" said Woo-Hoo to the attendant.

"Not until we are in the air and come by with the cart," she said.

He went back to the bottle in the seat back, taking another swig as the plane taxied out from the gate. "Vegas," he said as he put the water bottle back.

The plane took off and turned toward the southwest, and it wasn't long until we had leveled off, and the drink cart made its way down the aisle with refreshments. By the time the cart was at row eleven, my neighbor had finished half the bottle in the seat back and was really getting buzzed.

"What can I get you to drink?" the attendant asked Woo-Hoo.

"Double vodka and a PBR," he replied.

"How about a coffee?" I said under my breath while the guy put down the seat tray in front of the middle seat.

The flight attendant served the guy the drinks, which he downed before the refreshment cart had made it to the back of the plane. He was really getting trashed and stopped the cart as it was heading back to the front of the plane. "Can I get another round?" he asked.

The flight attendant could see that my neighbor was drunk and told him they would come back in a bit but needed to get the cart put away.

"Shit!" he said as the cart was pulled to the front of the plane. "Hey, man, you got some paper?" he asked me.

"You can't smoke on the plane," I said.

"No, man," he said. "Wanna show you something."

I pulled out a piece of copy paper I had in my backpack and handed it to him.

"This is wrong. Needs to be square," he said as he handed it back to me.

I folded the piece of paper so I could tear off enough to make it square, licked the edge, and tore off the piece. I handed it back to him.

"Watch this," he said as he took the paper and began to fold it over and over. He had to redo several of the folds because of his inebriation.

After forty-five minutes of folding and refolding, Woo-Hoo completed his art project, which looked like a childhood cootie catcher. He began to tell a story as he reshaped the paper over and over. "It's a house, now a boat, now a tie, and now a—press here." He held the paper shape toward me. His hands were shaking from the booze. "Press it," he said again.

"I don't know where," I said.

"In the middle. Press it," he said.

I pressed the middle of the shape, and nothing happened.

"Do it again!" he said.

I pressed harder, and the paper shape fell apart. He looked at me as if I had done something wrong and then laughed and pulled on the edges of the origami. The shape re-formed into a small box.

"Something to put luck into," he said. "I need some luck, man."

He put the paper box into the seat back as the aircraft began the descent into Las Vegas. He then took the last swig of the water bottle, crushed it, and put it back into the seat back. "I need some luck, man," he said again as he put his head on the window next to his seat, looking out at the Vegas Strip as we approached McCarran Airport.

After a smooth landing, we deplaned, and I followed the other passengers to the baggage claim. Suspended over the baggage area was a 1958 Cessna 172, which had set a record for endurance flying. For as many times as I had been to Las Vegas, I had never noticed the *Hacienda*-lettered Cessna. I could see Woo-Hoo waiting on the other side of the baggage carousel. He was clearly trying to stand without falling over while he waited for baggage.

As the baggage carousel began to drop out bags to the waiting passengers, I saw a lady with a hand-printed sign running toward us. She noticed the inebriated guy and started yelling, "Woo-hoo!" As she got closer, I could read what was on the sign: "Welcome home from prison, Larry!" He handed her the paper box he had made on the plane, and in turn, he received a hug. Maybe that reunion was the luck Larry had been hoping for.

I think some of the luck from Larry's origami box might have rubbed off on me, because I won a jackpot that night on the slots. Woo-hoo!

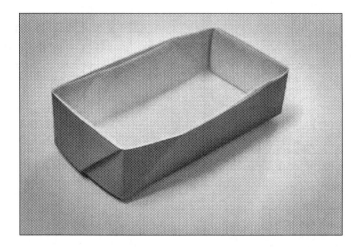

CHAPTER 9

NASHVILLE BOOGIE

Music City, USA—otherwise known as Nashville, Tennessee—had really lived up to its name for the three days I was in town for the National Warbird Operators Conference, or NWOC. The conference is an annual gathering of warbird pilots and industry experts to kick off the airshow season with an emphasis on safety. The conference includes some great speakers, small-group breakouts, camaraderie, and reflection on the highs and lows of operating vintage military aircraft.

One of the highlights of that year's conference was getting to visit the world-famous Printer's Alley and one of my favorite music venues: the Bourbon Street Blues and Boogie Bar.

I have an inner hillbilly that craves Cajun food and rockabilly music. I can't get enough of either, and the Bourbon Street Blues and Boogie

Bar didn't disappoint me on the last night of the conference. Shrimp and crawfish étouffée, along with cold beer and the driving music of the bar, wrapped up a fantastic three days. Music City was alive and well.

I was heading back to the reality of everyday life the next morning on a United flight from Nashville International Airport to Denver. It was sad, but my inner hillbilly would have to go into hibernation for a while.

The midmorning boarding process for the flight was smooth, and it wasn't long before I settled into seat 8A on the Airbus A319 jet. Shortly after I buckled in, an older gentleman sat in the middle seat next to me. He reminded me of a childhood hero of mine, Captain Kangaroo, complete with a bushy gray mustache and huge gray sideburns. He was wearing jeans, a red plaid shirt, and a beat-up straw fedora. He said hello as he took his seat and then pushed a pair of thick Coke-bottle-lensed glasses up his large drinker's nose. He proceeded to click his seat belt, cross his arms, and pull the front of his hat down in preparation for some sleep. "Long night," he said as he let out a sigh and pushed up his glasses again.

Boarding continued for the flight, and it looked as if the aisle seat in row eight might remain vacant so Captain could move over. However, the hope of some extra room faded when a young mom took the seat with her infant child in her arms. Captain remained still and didn't acknowledge that a crying baby and its mother were sitting next to him. The young mom organized her possessions under the seat in front of her and filled the seat back with baby goods as the main cabin door closed for takeoff.

The plane pushed back from the gate and taxied quickly to runway thirteen. Soon we were rotating toward the sky.

Next to me, Captain looked as if he had fallen asleep, and the baby next to him fell asleep too. The young mom gently rocked her baby as the jet climbed to the cruising altitude of thirty-four thousand feet.

The voice of the airline captain came on the overhead speaker: "Ladies and gentlemen, this is your captain. We have reached our cruising altitude. Air is smooth, so I am turning off the seat belt sign. Enjoy your flight."

At that moment, the stench of one of the worst farts I have ever smelled hit my face like a mustard-gas bomb.

"My God!" said the guy in the seat in front of me.

I couldn't breathe and put my shirt sleeve up to my face in an effort to filter the gas. It didn't help, and I swore it was getting worse. That was when I noticed Captain, with his eyes still closed, grin. He was the source of the fart that continued to disseminate row by row throughout the cabin.

"Ugh!"

"Holy crap!"

"Who shit their pants?"

Those were just a few of the comments as the smell hit the noses of nearby passengers.

The baby woke up and began to cry. At that time, Captain opened his eyes and said, "Smells like the baby needs a diaper change."

I knew better. He had probably soiled himself.

The young mom picked up the baby and smelled its bottom. "No, he's good," she said.

Then another wave hit.

"Come on, man!" said the guy in front of me. "Give us a break, and hit the head."

I thought for sure Captain would take the advice and go to the bathroom, but that would have indicated he had indeed let out the death farts. He would have to wait until a few other scapegoat bathroom users passed by, and the other passengers and I would have to fear for our lives for the next two hours.

As another silent, deadly fart hit, Captain pulled out a crusty cloth handkerchief and held it up to his bulbous nose. I thought he was making an effort to filter his own gas, but instead, he blew his nose onto the crunchy cloth and then proceeded to open up the handkerchief to see what he had made. Just to make sure he had cleaned out his nostrils, Captain placed his left pinkie finger in the cavern of an opening and twisted his fingernail around to scrape the edges. After examining what he had scraped out of his nose, he rubbed the boogers onto the handkerchief. It was simply disgusting.

He drilled out each side of his nose over the next hour, all the while gassing me and everyone else in the area.

As I suspected, after a few folks had come and gone to the bathroom, Captain asked the young mom if he could get out to use the facilities. *Thank God!* I thought to myself as he got up. I looked at the bottom of the seat he was sitting in to make sure he hadn't soiled himself. Fortunately for Captain, there wasn't any burned-out area or mystery stain on the seat.

Captain made his way to the front of the plane, toward the bathroom, and I thought a good bowel movement would stop the gas attack for the rest of the flight. But as Captain neared the bathroom, another horrible stench hit the air. "My God, man!" said the guy in front of me.

The young mom lifted her baby's bottom toward her nose. "Aw, you made a boom-boom," she said in a giggly voice to her baby. "Let's fix you up."

I felt bad for the young mom, knowing she would have to endure the toxic environment in the bathroom after Captain came back. But then she did something I had never seen on a flight. She put down the table in front of her and placed the baby on it.

No friggin' way, I thought to myself. *Yeah, she's going to do it.*

The mom reached into a diaper bag and pulled out a fresh pair of Huggies.

Soon a used nuclear-waste-smelling diaper was replaced with a new one. The baby was put back together just as Captain returned to his seat. The young mom returned the fold-down table to a locked position and got up to let Captain take his seat.

"Whew! That was a bad one," said Captain as he sat down. I didn't know if he meant what he had left in the bathroom or if he meant the baby diaper. He pulled out the nasty handkerchief and worked on his nose for the rest of the flight.

I curled up into a ball next to the window, shut my eyes, and tried to erase in my mind what I had witnessed on the flight. It didn't work. God, how I wished I were still in Nashville.

It smelled like a dirty diaper for the rest of the flight home until we landed in Denver, and I couldn't wait to get off the plane that day and breathe in some fresh Colorado air. The young mom left the dirty diaper in the seat pocket, and Captain used the nasty handkerchief again as he walked off the plane. It was gross to witness that guy blow his nose while he made his way up the Jetway, but I could have sworn he had a little boogie in his step.

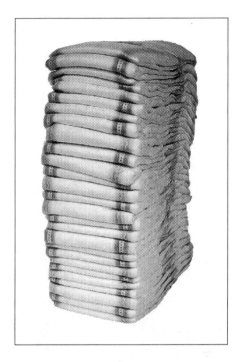

CHAPTER 10

DIVERT TO CASPER

The Experimental Aircraft Association, or EAA, is an international organization of airplane fanatics—like me—with more than two hundred thousand members worldwide. Since the EAA was founded in 1953 by Paul Poberezny and a group of like-minded friends, millions of visitors have gathered at the annual EAA AirVenture Oshkosh fly-in in Oshkosh, Wisconsin. It is one of my favorite events to attend. You will see more than half a million aviation enthusiasts there, along with more than ten thousand aircraft of all types coming and going over a week's time.

Weather always plays a part in the annual adventure. I had learned from previous trips to Oshkosh how to effectively get there and where to stay. One year, when I flew with my friend and partner, Dr. Michael Bertz, in a British Jet Provost, we were diverted by weather and had to land in Madison,

Wisconsin, where we sat for two days, waiting for a window in the storms to fly on to the big show. Another year, I flew into Green Bay, Wisconsin; drove to nearby Neenah, Wisconsin; and stayed in a fleabag motel that charged $199 a night for what was normally a $39-a-night room. There was a seven-night stay minimum, but I left after just two nights due to bed bugs and all-night parties happening in the room next to mine. I gladly left money on the table to get out of the situation. Camping is another option at Oshkosh, but the event has earned the nickname Sloshkosh thanks to what seems like an annual massive downpour occurring the first few days of the show. I have experienced some incredible rains at Oshkosh, which has kept me away from the campgrounds.

One year, I was to debut our TV show, *Chasing Planes*, at Oshkosh, and it was suggested I fly to Milwaukee, Wisconsin; rent a car; and drive an hour and a half to Wittman Regional Airport, where the fly-in is held. I took that suggestion and booked a flight to Milwaukee and then booked a room at a Hilton Garden Inn near the EAA. It was one of the smoothest travel experiences in my life, and the Oshkosh trip couldn't have been better that year. The TV show debut was a hit, and I saw hundreds of friends, watched some incredible aircraft fly, ate way too many cheese curds, drank a few beers, and walked more than fifty miles at AirVenture. Life was good.

My Oshkosh routine is pretty consistent, and that year was no different. I always make the last day of the EAA show a half day so I can beat the traffic. I get there early and walk five miles, from the warbirds in the north part of the field all the way to the antique planes in the south.

Around noon, I made the drive back to Billy Mitchell Airport in Milwaukee. The traffic was unusually light that day, and I made great time back to the Cream City.

After dropping off my rental car and checking in for the flight, I had time to visit the Mitchell Gallery of Flight museum, which is inside the main terminal area. It's a hidden gem of an aviation collection in Milwaukee's airport—and fewer calories than a last-minute beer and cheese curds.

I made my way through security and continued on to the departure gate, where a fifty-passenger Canadair Regional Jet, or CRJ, was connected to the Jetway. The tight cabin of a CRJ isn't one of my favorites to travel in, and I was a bit worried about being cramped in the plane for two hours. There are sets of two seats on the port side (left side) of the cabin and a single seat on the starboard (right side) of the cabin. I had a window seat for the flight to Denver, and the seating area was so small that I rested my left foot on top of a four-inch-tall ledge on the floor to give myself more room.

Before long, my concern turned from the tight airplane cabin to the weather brewing in the distance. Blackening skies to the west were in our path to Colorado, and previous flying experience told me that meant turbulence and other bad weather conditions. As we were about to board the small jet, I received a text message from my wife, who was in Denver: "Have you seen the weather? Bad hail predicted this afternoon."

Summer weather in Denver is predictable, namely afternoon thunderstorms, turbulence, and damaging hail that can be the size of a baseball. I knew the small size of the jet could make for a rough westbound ride.

I took my seat and cinched down my seat belt in preparation for the possibility of a bumpy flight and was quickly joined by a lady in the seat next to me. She looked to be in her midfifties, with long brown hair that had streaks of gray every so often. She seemed frail and wore jeans and a short-sleeved T-shirt, and she clasped a windbreaker as she took her seat.

"Hi there," she said as she looked for her seat belt. "Do you fly much?"

"I fly all the time. Why?" I replied.

"This is only my second time on a plane," she said.

"When was the first?" I asked.

"Three days ago, when I came out to Milwaukee to see my mom. Had to put her in assisted living," she said. "I am really scared to fly."

"I'm a pilot, so I can tell you that this plane is safe, and you will be fine," I told her. "You don't need to be scared unless I am scared. Then we have a problem."

Her eyes got big at my statement, and her hands shook as she attached the seat belt ends together.

"We'll be fine. Really," I said as I lifted my leg to put my foot on the small ledge on the floor.

Boarding was brief, as there were only about thirty passengers on the flight. While we pushed back from the gate, the left engine was started. Soon the right engine started, and I could see the wing spoilers go up and down as part of the preflight check before we taxied out for takeoff.

"Hey, are you sure this is a safe plane?" asked the lady next to me. "It is way smaller than the one I took the other day."

"I fly these types of planes all the time," I said. "What's your name?"

"Janet," she said. "You must be Gordon."

"How would you know that?" I asked.

"It says on your name tag." She pointed at the EAA name tag I had forgotten to take off when I left Oshkosh that morning.

"Thought you were a psychic for a minute," I said as I took off the name tag and put it in the seat back.

Janet was visibly shaking as the jet lined up for takeoff.

"You will be fine, Janet," I said as power was added, and we began down the runway.

She closed her eyes and held on tightly to both armrests. Immediately after takeoff, the jet encountered turbulence, and Janet's grip tightened in an effort to hold on. She let out a yelp as some moderate turbulence shook the plane.

"How long is this going to last?" she asked.

"It will be okay, Janet. They will try to find smooth air. I promise," I said just as another jolt shook the plane.

"I knew it was a bad idea to fly," she said. "I had a vision, but I had to help my mom."

As I was about the say something, the captain of the flight made an announcement: "Ladies and gentlemen, this is your captain. We are expecting some turbulence on the flight this afternoon and have asked our flight attendant to stay seated. We need you to stay seated and keep your seat belts on. We will try to find some smoother air, but Denver is reporting some heavy wind and hail for later. We will keep you informed. Thanks for flying with us today."

"Are we going to be okay?" asked Janet.

"Yeah, they know what they are doing up there," I told her. "At least I hope so," I said to myself as the plane rocked to the left.

I could see the sky in front of us getting darker as the plane continued to shake. Janet kept her eyes closed and hung on to the armrests as the flight continued westward.

Continuous turbulence kept everyone in his or her seat for the next hour. Despite the seat belt sign being on for safety, several passengers left their seats to use the bathroom. The flight attendant, who had remained seated during the entire flight, reminded passengers that the seat belt sign was on and asked them to remain seated, but the bladders of some passengers made them take a chance and make a dash for relief.

Over the next thirty minutes, the turbulence went from moderate to occasionally severe conditions. The plane would lose a thousand or more feet in altitude in an instant because of downdrafts, which shook the plane and caused passengers to scream. Janet held on for dear life and kept glancing at me to see if I was in control of the situation.

"Are we still okay?" she asked just as another downdraft hit the plane.

"Honestly, I am going to be shocked if we make it to Denver," I said.

"Are we going to crash?" she said in a high-pitched voice.

"No, I think we are going to get diverted because of weather," I said just as the overhead voice of the captain came on.

"Folks, this is your captain. As you can tell, the weather is not cooperating today. Flights in and out of Denver are on hold because of a storm over the airport, so we are going to have to divert," he said. "We'll keep you updated."

"What does that mean?" asked Janet.

"They are not going to land in Denver and will go to an alternate airport," I replied.

"Where?" she asked.

"Not sure, but it's the right decision," I said.

The plane made a right turn and headed to the northwest as turbulence continued to rock the aircraft. Ahead of us was a break in the black skies, and rays of sunshine came through the clouds like a spotlight to safety. Soon we were descending toward the ground, and the air outside stabilized, so the plane stopped shaking. The CRJ wing spoilers helped the plane descend faster, and fifteen minutes later, the flaps and landing gear were extended. I had no idea where we were about to land, but the surrounding terrain looked like rural Wyoming.

As the plane touched down, the flight attendant announced on the overhead speaker that we were in Casper, Wyoming. She asked the passengers to remain seated until the plane came to a final stop.

As the CRJ taxied into the ramp area of the Casper airport, the captain made an announcement: "Ladies and gentlemen, welcome to Casper, Wyoming. We plan to sit here for a while until the weather gets better in Denver. Feel free to get up and use the bathroom, but we won't be leaving the plane."

A dozen passengers unclicked their seat belts and made a dash to the single bathroom in the rear of the plane.

"What will happen next?" asked Janet.

"Hopefully, the weather will clear out in Denver, and we will get going soon," I said.

The captain came back onto the overhead. "Folks, we are going to try to get out of here in the next forty-five minutes. Our shift times are coming up, so we need to be in the air in the next hour, or we will have to fly in some new pilots," he said. "We'll keep you informed."

"What does that mean?" said Janet.

"It means we might have to spend the night here," I replied. I had been through that type of travel situation before, and my instincts told me to get prepared to spend the night in Casper. "We'll be fine," I told Janet with hope in my voice.

Thirty minutes went by before another announcement from the captain. "Folks, weather has moved out in Denver, and we need you to take your seats so we can get going."

Several people had not gotten to use the bathroom but angrily took their seats again. Soon the engines of the CRJ started, and all looked good to get back in the air—until the wing spoiler preflight check occurred. Just as I had seen in Milwaukee, the crew extended the wing spoilers to test them prior to taxiing out to the runway, but the spoilers didn't retract back into the wing. I could hear clunking in the mechanism as the crew tried over and over to get the spoilers back down into the wing.

It didn't work, and soon the captain was back on the overhead. "Sorry, folks, but we are having trouble with the spoilers on the wing and will have to return to the terminal and deplane. We will get maintenance to take a look at it as soon as possible."

Janet looked confused at the situation. "What's going to happen?" she asked.

"We're all spending the night in Casper," I answered.

Janet started to cry. "I knew something bad was going to happen. I don't know what to do," she said.

A voice came on the overhead speaker. "Please see the gate agent as you deplane, and we will book you on another flight."

After a short taxi to the small terminal, the engines shut down, and the door of the CRJ opened to let the passengers out. Most of them ran to the bathrooms in the terminal after deplaning. I told Janet to stick near me as I pulled out my cell phone and called the airline. The other passengers formed a long line at the gate agent desk to rebook their flights, and the flight crew exited the airport with bags in hand.

I learned from my call to the airline that there would be no flights from Casper to Denver for two more days, as the weather had really backed up the airline system. Instead of joining the gate agent line to rebook my travel, I asked Janet where she lived and how she was getting home. She told me that her husband had dropped her off at the Denver airport for her trip to Wisconsin.

"I just want to get home, and I'm scared to fly again," she said.

I could tell she was distraught, and I thought about some options for both of us that didn't involve two days in Casper waiting for a flight home.

"I have a plan B, and you are more than welcome to join me," I told Janet. "I know you don't like to fly, so how about driving?"

"You seem to know what you are doing, so okay," she said.

"Follow me," I said, grabbing my bag.

There was a lone agent at the Avis rental car counter as I walked up and asked if they had any cars.

"One left," said the agent.

I pulled out my driver's license and credit card. "I'll take it, and can I make this a one-way rental and drop it off at the Denver airport?" I asked.

"Two-hundred-dollar extra charge," said the agent.

"Done," I said as I slipped him my credit card.

Three and a half hours of driving got me and my passenger, Janet, to the rental car return at Denver International Airport. My plan B had saved two or more days of waiting for a mechanic or replacement airplane so we could get back to Colorado. Plan B had also saved a nervous flier from the anxiety of travel unknowns. Janet was happy to have made the last part of her trip in a car that didn't shake from turbulence. Her husband met us at the Avis car rental facility and thanked me for helping out. I was happy to help someone in need and happy to be home, and I didn't let a little weather ruin a great trip. It's all part of the misadventures of flying.

CHAPTER 11

MAX THE DOG

The Navy Cross is the United States military's second-highest decoration awarded for valor in combat and is awarded primarily to members of the United States Navy, Marine Corps, and Coast Guard for extraordinary heroism.

One of the recipients of the Navy Cross is former Navy SEAL Marcus Luttrell, who also received the Purple Heart for his actions in June 2005 against Taliban fighters during Operation Red Wings. During the operation, his Special Reconnaissance element of four was discovered by local herdsman, they were ambushed, and all were killed except for Marcus

Luttrell. Luttrell had a number of fractures, a broken back, and numerous shrapnel wounds. The story of Operation Red Wings is featured in the movie *Lone Survivor*. Despite the injuries he suffered, Marcus Luttrell returned to active duty and was deployed to fight again in Operation Iraqi Freedom in 2006. He had his knees blown out and fractured his spine, which led to his discharge from the navy. He is a true American hero.

I had the opportunity to hear Marcus Luttrell tell his story at the University of Colorado's Macky Auditorium and was amazed by his story, his encouragement of others, and his commitment to his country. I was also amazed by a Labrador retriever named Rigby that sat quietly at Luttrell's side during his talk. His new service dog had taken the place of his beloved Dasy, a Labrador retriever that had been shot and killed by an asshole in Texas, who was found guilty and later convicted of animal cruelty.

Seeing how Rigby supported Marcus Luttrell gave me an incredible appreciation for service dogs and the role they play to support individuals with disabilities.

The definition of a service dog has certainly changed over the years when it comes to air travel. People have taken liberties with the Americans with Disabilities Act (ADA) definition of the role of a service dog and now bring emotional support animals and comfort animals into airports and onto airplanes.

The ADA says it does not matter if a person has a note from a doctor stating that he or she has a disability and needs to have the animal for emotional support. A doctor's letter does not turn an animal into a service animal, but rather than enforce the definition of a service dog, the airlines have allowed various animals, such as rats, pigs, cats, peacocks, and even horses, onto flights. Personally, I have seen snakes, tarantulas, chickens, ferrets, a duck, ant farms, and even a bee hive on a flight. It's crazy.

Sitting in the gate area of SeaTac Airport was a young man wearing large headphones and holding an extendable leash attached to a forty-pound black

Portuguese water dog. The dog was cute and would occasionally walk away from the owner, who had not locked the extendable leash. The owner was immersed in his music and had his eyes closed while bobbing his head to the beat of the tunes. He was oblivious whenever his dog pulled out his leash and wandered over to passengers sitting in the seats across from him. Occasionally, the owner would open his eyes and realize his dog was not at his side.

"Max, come here," he would say as he tugged the leash with his hand.

Max would reluctantly come back to his owner, who would again close his eyes and go back to the beat of his music. Max did not have on a red vest to indicate he was service dog or even the blue vest of an emotional support dog. Max was just a dog that was along for the ride.

Across the gate area was an older lady in an airport wheelchair waiting for the boarding process for the flight to Denver to begin. An airport employee stood by to push the lady onto the plane. The lady had both of her arms wrapped around a large bag that sat on her lap. She would occasionally open the top of the bag, quickly look inside, and then shut the bag tightly again, as if to keep something from jumping out.

As the gate agent made an announcement that boarding would begin in ten minutes, the young man who sat with Max took out a brush from a backpack and began to run the brush through the dog's hair. Max did not seem to enjoy the brushing and tried to nip at the brush several times in an effort to stop the process.

Max's owner stopped brushing after he had a large ball of hair in his lap. He stood up and said, "Let's go, Max," leaving his backpack and luggage sitting unprotected on the seat next to him. Max and his owner left the gate area to an unknown location as the boarding process began.

The old lady with the large bag was pushed onto the plane first, along with other passengers with disabilities and parents with young children. Next were military passengers, followed by the elite mileage members who spent their lives on airline flights. I boarded the flight shortly after and took my seat in 10A, behind the row with the old lady, who was sitting in 9B with the large bag, which was now on the floor between her legs. The boarding process continued and was about to conclude, when the young guy with Max the dog got on the plane. They took a seat next to me in 10B after the young guy put his backpack and luggage in the overhead bin. Max sniffed my hand as the young guy put him in between his legs. Max was restless, and his handler did not make an effort to calm him down. Max sniffed the hand of the lady in the aisle seat, and his owner finally took off his headphones and said, "Max, calm down." Max lay on the floor as the flight attendants came down the aisle to make their final checks prior to takeoff.

Max stayed mostly calm as the plane rolled back, started up, and taxied out to the runway for takeoff. The jet lined up and added power, and we roared down the runway at SeaTac Airport before rotating for a smooth takeoff and climb out for the two-and-a-half-hour flight to Denver.

Max remained on the floor in front of his owner during the flight and kept his head under the seat where the old lady sat. She had fallen asleep as the plane settled into a cruising altitude of thirty-three thousand feet.

Shortly after the drink cart had made its way down the aisle to serve the passengers, I noticed Max was becoming agitated under the seat. He seemed to be gnawing on something. I looked at his owner; he had his headphones back on, and his eyes were closed. Max continued to chew on something, and suddenly, the old lady in seat 9B woke up. "What are you doing? Not my chicken!" she yelled as she tried to pull up her bag from the floor. Max had a grip on it with his teeth and did not let go.

The young guy, who was half-asleep and still listening to music, felt Max's commotion at his feet and, without opening his eyes, said, "Max, calm down."

The old lady kept trying to pull her bag up, saying, "Stop it! Stop it! Not my chicken!"

Max finally let go of the bag and wiggled out from under the seat. His owner did not budge or open his eyes.

Max had a mouthful of feathers and was chewing the remains of something as the old lady pulled the bag into her lap, opened it, and saw that something was missing. "No! Not my chicken! I need it for the ceremony," she said, freaking out.

Max finished eating whatever had been in the bag as his owner finally opened his eyes to see what was going on in the seat in front of him.

"Max, where did you get that feather?" said his owner as he pulled a chicken feather out of the corner of Max's mouth. He put the feather in the seat back pocket and then closed his eyes and went back to his music.

The old lady continued to freak out, and a flight attendant came to her row to see what was happening.

"Ma'am, what is wrong?" asked the attendant.

"The dog ate my chicken!" she said, still very agitated.

The attendant looked at our row and examined Max the dog. "Ma'am, the dog isn't doing anything, just lying on the floor," she said.

"He ate my voodoo chicken!" said the old lady. "I need the chicken."

"I wish there was something I could do," replied the flight attendant. "Sorry about that." With that, she walked away to prepare the cabin for landing.

The old lady sobbed while looking into her bag for the rest of the flight.

Max the dog looked happy. His owner slept through the landing.

The old lady was helped off the plane by wheelchair in Denver and looked to be casting a spell on Max's owner as he left the gate area. Max and his owner stopped by a water fountain as they were about to head through the terminal. The owner pulled out a small red vest from his backpack and put it on Max. It was a service dog vest, which had probably been taken off when Max got his brushing. Max had certainly done his job of keeping his owner calm that day, and maybe he also kept his owner safe from a voodoo hex.

I stopped by Chick-fil-A on the way out of the airport. For some reason, chicken sounded good.

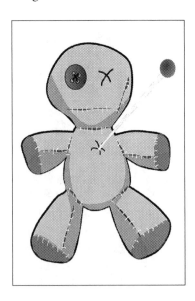

CHAPTER 12

MR. PEANUT

The Battle of Britain was one of the most significant and documented military campaigns of World War II. The Royal Air Force used Supermarine Spitfires and Hawker Hurricane fighter aircraft to help defend the United Kingdom against large-scale bombing attacks by the German Luftwaffe air force, which were intended to get Britain to agree to a peace settlement. The British knew better than to submit to Nazi Germany and continuously fought over the skies of the United Kingdom for nearly four months to defend air superiority over the Germans. The Battle of Britain is known as the first major German defeat in World War II and was a crucial turning point in the conflict to protect the United Kingdom.

The Supermarine Spitfire has always been a favorite airplane of mine. The beauty of the elliptical wings and the sound of the Rolls-Royce Merlin V-12 engine make it a desirable warbird for collectors around the world to own and fly.

My job of appraising warbirds and collectible aircraft brought an opportunity to go to London, England, to inspect and appraise a rare Mk IX Spitfire housed at London Biggin Hill Airport. Biggin Hill was a vital airfield during World War II, as it was one of the commanding bases for the Battle of Britain, with both Spitfires and Hurricanes from a variety of squadrons based there. Amazingly, Spitfires and Hurricanes are still operated at Biggin Hill, and the general public can fly in one of these historic fighters at the Biggin Hill Heritage Hangar. Imagine flying over the White Cliffs of Dover in a Spitfire. It would be the flight of a lifetime.

The flight from Denver to London Heathrow Airport is a solid nine hours in the air, which is half the time of the longest international flight I have ever taken. My client for the Spitfire inspection wanted to meet early the next morning, so I took a 3:55 p.m. flight that would arrive at Heathrow around seven o'clock the next morning. I have taken overnight flights in the past and have to admit I can never get in a good night's sleep. It amazes me how people can sleep for hours while crunched up in a small space on a plane. Of course, that isn't the case if you are in the front of the plane in a private first-class cocoon. I wasn't up front for my flight to London on a Boeing 757, which sits three passengers in a row on either side of the plane.

I was in seat 21A for the nine-hour ride to London, and I had plans to watch a few movies before getting some sleep if possible. It was going to be a long day in London after flying all night, so I really needed to try to get some rest.

The boarding process for the flight went smoothly, and the passenger seats were only half-filled by the time the main cabin door closed. Despite the light load for the flight, a middle-aged British guy took seat 21B. He was overweight and wore thick-rimmed glasses. He had on a pair of black sweatpants, a gray hooded sweatshirt, and a pair of camouflage Crocs shoes with no socks. As he sat down, he shoved a duffel bag under the seat in front of him and then asked how I was as he fell solidly into his seat.

"How's it going?" he said in a thick British accent.

"Doing great, thanks," I said just as he pulled his duffel bag out from under the seat.

"Forgot me snack," he said as he pulled out a large plastic container of peanuts. "Discovered Costco this trip," he added as he twisted off the top of the container. He reached into the container and pulled out a generous handful of peanuts that he shoved into his mouth. He crunched up the nuts and then proceeded to lick off his fingers one by one.

"Love these things," he said as he grabbed another handful. "Plenty here. Want some?" He offered me the container.

"No, thanks. I just ate," I said politely. In my head, I thought about his moist fingers he had just placed into the peanuts. I also thought about where his hands might have been prior to reaching into the container.

"Well, let me know," he replied as he continued to shove handful after handful of peanuts into his mouth. He licked his fingers and wiped them off on his sweatshirt after each handful he ate. "Nuff for now," he said as the plane pushed back, and the engines started. He put the container back into his duffel bag and shoved it under the seat.

It was beginning to get dark as the 757 taxied out to runway nine at Denver International and took off to the east, toward the United Kingdom. After an uneventful climb to our cruising altitude, the seat belt light was extinguished, and passengers began to move about the cabin.

"Wonder if I can move over there," said the Brit, pointing to the empty row of seats across from us.

"No reason not to," I told him.

He unbuckled his seat belt, grabbed his duffel bag, and stood up. "That is great. Need my sleep tonight," he said as he moved across the aisle.

It wasn't long before flight attendants made their way through the cabin to offer drinks and a meal service. The Brit who sat across from me went back to his giant container of peanuts after the meal service, watching a movie on the monitor in front of him.

I thought, *My God, is that guy Mr. Peanut? How can he eat so many?*

As the guy took another handful toward his mouth, an announcement came on the overhead speakers from the female purser.

"Ladies and gentlemen, we will be turning off the lights so people can sleep, so please use the light above your seat if you need to," said the purser. "We will be offering a light breakfast when we are closer to London. Thanks for flying today."

As the cabin darkened, passengers around me reclined their seats, covered themselves with the airline blankets, and positioned the small airline pillows in preparation to get some sleep.

That was when I noticed Mr. Peanut reach into his duffel bag and pull out a small kitchen hand towel. It was about a foot in width and two feet in length, and the age and wear of the fabric made it almost see-through.

Mr. Peanut slipped off his camo Crocs and then did something I had never seen. He pulled the hooded sweatshirt over his head and took it off, exposing his hairy bare chest and beer belly. He placed the old kitchen towel over his midsection and proceeded to pull down the black sweatpants and take them off. The transparency of the kitchen towel made it obvious that Mr. Peanut did not have on underwear. He balled up the sweatshirt and sweatpants into a makeshift pillow and pushed them into the corner of the window seat of the row he was sitting in. He held on to one corner of the kitchen towel as he lay down on the three seats in the row. He rolled onto his right side and placed his head on his clothes. The bottoms of his dirty bare feet were pointed my way.

What the hell? Seriously? I thought as the nude guy began snoring.

I tried to shield my eyes by placing my right hand up to my forehead, but the damage was done. The sight of Mr. Peanut had been burned into my mind.

I woke up when the cabin lights came back on about an hour outside London. I had somehow fallen asleep while watching a movie to distract myself from what I had seen earlier.

I cautiously looked over to the aisle across from me, and to my surprise, Mr. Peanut was redressed and working on the Costco container again as he watched something on his monitor.

I thought I might have dreamed what I had witnessed, but then I noticed the small kitchen towel sitting on the seat next to the guy. It really had happened.

After landing in London, the other passengers and I gathered our belongings and slowly made our way out of the plane and toward customs. Mr. Peanut shuffled his way through the airport in front of me. He looked to have had the good night of sleep he had wished for in Denver.

I would never be able to look at a jar of peanuts the same way again.

CHAPTER 13

YOU'RE CHECKING WHAT?

The September 11, 2001, attacks on the United States not only killed nearly three thousand people but also forever changed the way people travel, especially by air.

The Transportation Security Administration, or TSA, was formed in response to the September 11 attacks, and screening of passengers at airports by TSA employees is now a way of life. The TSA screens millions of passengers and baggage at more than 450 US airports each year and keeps passengers safe by using screening officers, federal air marshals, and mobile teams of dog handlers leading dogs that can sniff out explosives and other contraband.

Despite this advanced security system, it is incredible to see what people still try to bring with them through security.

October had been a brutal month of cold weather and snow in the Front Range of Colorado. A full foot of snow had fallen, and the temperature was a frigid eleven degrees when I got in my car to make the drive to Denver International Airport (DIA) for a trip to Austin, Texas. Only a few weeks before, we'd had glorious sunshine and blue skies in Louisville, Colorado. Old Man Winter had made an early appearance, and it looked as if he was going to stick around for a while in the Denver area. I was looking forward to the warm weather in Texas.

Traffic on the Northwest Parkway to the airport was awful. Ice had formed on the road, and blowing snow made for bad visibility. My wipers worked hard to keep snow and ice off my windshield as I slowly made the forty-mile trip to DIA. Several cars had slid from the highway into ditches after losing traction, which made me focus harder and drive slower than usual to the airport. The weather and slow traffic were working against me to make my flight on time. I knew that security would have to move fast for me to get to the gate before the boarding process ended and the door to the plane was closed.

A normally forty-five-minute drive turned into an hour and a half by the time I was in the airport parking structure. Murphy's law was working against me that morning. Not only was the drive unusually long, but every spot in the parking structure was full. I drove around and around and then up and down several levels until I finally spotted a guy pulling his luggage through the structure. I stalked him by slowly driving behind him and hoped he would be quick to vacate his parking spot for my car. He walked with a cell phone to his ear as he looked around for his car. The clock was ticking for me.

"Come on, man!" I said out loud in my car.

He continued at a slow pace through the parking area, stopping every few cars to look around to see where his car might be. He was in no hurry.

I continued to slowly follow behind him until he began a fast walk to the stairwell of the parking garage.

I rolled my window down and asked, "Hey, can I get your spot?"

He put the cell phone down to his chest and said, "I'm up a level."

He put his phone back to his ear and began walking up the stairs. I, in turn, spun my tires as I turned my car toward the ramp of the parking level above.

After a quick drive to the upper level, I caught up and followed the guy again. His car was parked in a spot that could not have been farther away from the airport terminal. The clock continued to tick.

I waited while the guy searched for his keys as he continued his phone call. He located the keys after what seemed forever, unlocked the car, and then slowly put his luggage in the backseat. "Ticktock," I said to myself.

Finally, the car started, and the guy backed his car out, leaving a space for me. By then, two other cars had stopped on the other side to try to swipe the space. I honked to alert them that I had been waiting for the spot, and I hoped they had the courtesy to move on. Fortunately, the spot was mine after the guy left, and I pulled in quickly, shut off the car, grabbed my bag, and ran toward the terminal while my breath froze in the cold. It was tight, but if security was fast, I would make my flight and be on a plane soon to the warmth of Texas.

After running as fast as I could while pulling my luggage, I arrived at the security-check line and took my spot behind an older guy wearing a brown wool overcoat and a brown ivy-style hat. He pulled a black piece of luggage behind him as we slowly advanced through the security line.

Ticktock, I said in my head as I looked at a large wall clock, which indicated I had just twenty minutes to make my gate before boarding ended.

After passing a TSA agent who checked my identification and ticket, I rejoined the guy in the brown overcoat and quickly placed my baggage on the inspection rollers leading to screening equipment. The old guy in front of me struggled to put his black bag on the rollers. I offered to help him, but he became agitated at my offer and then guarded his bag.

"I have it," he said as he placed the bag on the rollers.

His bag made its way into the screening machine, and I pushed my bag against his and then took my place to walk through the body scanner. I looked at the clock again: fifteen minutes until boarding ended.

I walked through the body scanner after the old man had gone before me. He slowly walked over to where our bags would exit while I prepared to grab my bag and run once it popped out.

The TSA agent sitting next to the monitor of the screening machine cocked his head to one side as the screening machine belt stopped. He leaned in to look closer at the contents of what was on the screen. He then leaned back and yelled at another TSA agent to join him. The clock continued to tick.

As the second TSA agent arrived, the first agent pointed at something on the monitor. The second agent gazed at the monitor, and then he too cocked his head at what he saw.

"Whose black bag is this?" said the second agent. He pulled out the black bag the old man had placed on the belt.

"Be careful with that," said the old man as the agent put the luggage in front of him.

"How about this bag?" asked the TSA agent as he pulled my black bag out of the luggage scanner.

"That would be mine," I said, raising my hand.

"Both of you follow me," said the agent as he grabbed the bags by the handles and walked to an inspection table. I had only ten minutes to spare before I missed my flight, and I still had to take a train to the departure gate.

The TSA agent placed the two bags on separate tables and then asked another TSA agent to join him. "You take a look at his," said the first agent to the other, pointing to my bag. He looked at me and said, "Your bag is just a random." He then looked at the old man and said, "Just what in the hell is in your bag?"

As he began to unzip the old man's bag, the elderly guy said, "Be careful."

My bag was already well under inspection when the TSA agent working with the old man pulled up the unzipped top. "What the hell? Is this what I think it is?" said the agent.

I looked over to see what the agent was talking about. It looked like a human head wrapped in plastic.

"You have some paperwork for this?" asked the agent.

"No, that is why I am personally carrying it," responded the old man.

"Man, you can't bring that thing through here!" said the agent. He got on his radio and asked for another agent to join him as he closed the zippered top of the bag.

"You're good to go," said the TSA agent who had inspected my bag.

"Great," I replied as I looked at the clock on the wall while grabbing my bag.

I didn't have time to stick around to see if what the old man had was really what I thought it was, so I hustled toward the escalator that went down to the trains.

After the extra time for the random baggage check, I felt it would be impossible to make my flight that day.

The door to the Jetway for the flight to Austin, Texas, closed just as I arrived at the gate, and the next flight to Austin was four hours later. Instead of being upset, I didn't lose my head over the wait that day.

CHAPTER 14

BIG SKY GAMBLE

The Big Sky Country of Montana has some of the most picturesque scenery in the world. The diverse terrain of Montana ranges from the Rocky Mountains to the Great Plains. It is a vast area of land that includes Glacier National Park and wilderness preserves that go all the way into Canada. It is a beautiful state that includes world-class hunting and fishing, stunning snowcapped peaks, skiing, deep blue lakes, and incredible wildlife.

Montana also has authorized limited legal gambling. There are seven federally recognized tribes that own ten casinos in Montana. There are also four small Indian gaming businesses on tribal lands and more than one hundred state-licensed electronic gaming casinos with gaming devices that play video poker, video keno, and video bingo. Many of these video gaming establishments are in truck stops, restaurants, bars, and even the occasional Laundromat. There is no live house gaming in the state, such as roulette, but I thought differently as I took a gamble on one of my trips to the Treasure State.

Helena, the capital of Montana, has a rich past. It was founded in 1864 during the Montana gold rush. Wealth was accumulated during the gold rush, which contributed to the building of some beautiful Victorian neighborhoods in Helena, which is the fifth-least-populated state capital in the United States. Stephen Ambrose, historian and author of *Band of Brothers* and *Undaunted Courage*, two of my favorite books, lived in Helena, Montana. Another notable figure from the Helena area was Ted Kaczynski, a.k.a. the Unabomber, who lived in a small cabin in nearby Lincoln, Montana. The FBI used Helena as the site to coordinate the capture and arrest of the Unabomber. Kaczynski is now serving eight life sentences in a supermax prison in Florence, Colorado.

I had never been to Helena and was surprised to get a call from a former colleague who invited me to visit and interview for a sales position at a software company that was expanding nationwide. The position and opportunity to visit the state capital of Montana intrigued me, so I accepted the invitation to travel to Helena.

My former colleague said the company was raising money to expand the sales team, so to save on travel expenses, they were using a small airline based in Billings, Montana, called Big Sky Airlines. I had accumulated some frequent flier miles and could have made the trip without any expense to the company, but my airline did not fly to Helena from Denver. They did, however, fly to Billings, so I booked a flight there using my miles, and the company booked me on a Big Sky flight from Billings to Helena.

I didn't know much about Big Sky Airlines at the time, so I asked my colleague, Mark, what to expect.

"Oh, I wouldn't expect much," Mark said. "It's certainly not a big plane, but it should get you here."

He would not go into any other details about flying Big Sky Airlines to Helena but said he looked forward to seeing me.

Three days later, I was on a United Boeing 737 flight from Denver to

Billings. The flight was only an hour long and without incident. As the jet approached Billings, snow began to fall, and the visibility was such that you could not see the ground or the surrounding town, much less Billings Logan Airport. Five miles from the airport, the jet's landing gear came down, and two minutes later, we touched down on the runway of the Billings airport. A short taxi put the Boeing 737 at the small terminal, and soon after, I deplaned through a Jetway with the other passengers.

There were only a few gates at the Billings terminal, so it was a quick walk to the passenger waiting area for Big Sky Airlines. As I arrived at the gate for the flight to Helena, I could see a waiting nineteen-seat Swearingen Metroliner on the outside ramp area behind the gate agent desk. Passengers would have to board the aircraft by walking outside and up the stairs of the turboprop plane.

The snow began to fall in heavy, wet flakes as passengers watched through the glass windows in the gate area. The flakes were so big and fluffy that it looked as if a giant pillow fight were going on at the Billings airport. As I watched the flakes come down, a voice came over the speaker in the passenger waiting area.

"Folks, as you can see, the snow is really coming down out there. We will have to deice the plane before we get going, so please stand by for more announcements about when we will begin boarding," said the gate agent.

In the distance, I could see a pickup truck with a large metal stairway in its bed slowly drive in the snow toward the plane. I continued to watch the snow fall while I tried to figure out what was going to happen next as the truck neared the back of the plane.

"Excuse me," said a middle-aged lady. "Are you one of the pilots?"

"No," I replied. "Why do you ask?"

"The tag on your luggage says *Crew*."

"Oh, that's from flight training. I'm a pilot, but I don't fly for the airlines," I said.

"I was really hoping you were with this flight. It's my first flight ever," she said. "I am really, really scared."

"I wouldn't be scared," I assured her.

"What about the snow? Is it okay to fly in this weather?" she asked.

"That's why they are deicing," I said, pointing to the pickup truck pulling up to the tail of the plane.

However, the truck didn't stop, and the metal stairs ran into the horizontal stabilizer of the plane. I watched in dismay as the guy driving the pickup got out and examined what had just happened.

"Is that supposed to happen?" asked the lady.

"No, I am sure we aren't going to be flying in that plane today," I told her as I shook my head in disbelief.

The snow continued to come down harder as the gate agent made another announcement.

"Folks, we need to swap planes due to a mechanical issue, so bear with us as we get another aircraft for today's flight," said the agent.

In the distance, I could see another Metroliner being pulled out of a hangar by a tug. It slowly made its way to the ramp area.

In my head, I began to question if I should take a chance with my personal safety after what I had witnessed. *I could rent a car to drive to Helena*, I thought.

"I'm really scared," said the lady again.

"Hey, if I am getting on the plane, we will be okay. You don't need to be scared unless I am scared," I replied.

In reality, I too was beginning to feel a bit scared as I watched the tug pull away the damaged plane. The tug took the broken Metroliner to the hangar from which the new plane had emerged.

The pickup with the metal stairwell was positioned behind the new plane, and the driver got out and climbed the stairs with what looked like a garden hose in his hand. Once he was at the top of the stairs, he began to spray liquid onto the surfaces of the plane as the snow continued to cover the area.

I was seriously thinking about walking out of the terminal, when another overhead announcement was made.

"Ladies and gentlemen, we are about to begin boarding to Helena. We will be going out the door next to the counter and out to the plane. Watch your step as you walk outside," said the agent.

"Will you help me onto the plane?" asked the lady.

I hesitated and thought about telling her we shouldn't fly that day. Something didn't feel right to me.

Against my own better judgment, I agreed to help the lady outside and onto the plane.

We walked to the plane as the huge snowflakes soaked any clothing they fell on. One of the two pilots for the flight was waiting at the stairs to the plane, reminding people to watch their step as they boarded. He was young and looked as if he had just graduated high school.

"Hey, you can sit in the jump seat today since you are crew," he said to me, pointing at my crew tag.

I accepted the invitation to sit in the jump seat and assured the lady I had helped out to the plane that the flight would be safe.

As I buckled into the jump seat, the pilot who had helped everyone onto the plane handed me a set of headphones. "Here you go! Glad you're on board today," he said, and he took the copilot seat.

In the left seat of the cockpit, another young guy was going through a preflight checklist. "Going to be bumpy," he said. "Quick turn too, since the other plane is out."

The door was closed, and the engines started on the twin turboprop. Soon we were taxiing out to the runway I had earlier landed on in a spacious 737 jet. For this flight, I was in what has been affectionately nicknamed the Sewer Tube.

"What's your schedule like?" the pilot asked the copilot as we taxied past the terminal building.

"Mine sucks. Can't wait for my interview next week," said the copilot. "When's yours?"

"Two weeks," said the pilot as the plane stopped short of the runway.

The tower cleared the plane for takeoff, and we taxied onto the runway. Power was added to the noisy Garrett engines, and soon the plane was piercing the falling snow as it climbed to the west.

I continued to listen to the flight crew complain about their schedules and other drama on the headset. Apparently, they had forgotten I was listening in, based on the way they were bitching. The conversation went on all the way until the plane began a descent to land.

The snow had stopped as we approached the Helena area, and I could now see the surrounding terrain and the town of Helena, with its domed capitol building, in the distance. The crew continued the descent, complaining in between radio transmissions with the Helena airport tower. The landing gear came down. They were setting up to land—but it wasn't the Helena airport they were preparing to land at. Helena was still ten miles away.

As the crew continued a straight-in approach to land, I got on the microphone of the headset and said, "Guys, I think the airport is twenty degrees to the right and ten miles away."

They looked at each other in disbelief as they remembered I was on the headset, and then they looked out the windscreen of the plane to the area of the actual Helena airport. Power was added, and the landing gear was brought back up into the wings of the plane. A gradual turn was made toward Helena's airport. The crew were silent until talking with the Helena tower again, this time to line up for landing at the right airport.

The lady who had been scared in Billings got off the plane in Helena with the other passengers, who had no idea they could have been deplaning at the wrong airport that day. She thanked me for assuring her the plane was safe. As I got off the plane, the two pilots asked if I was with the FAA and apologized for the possible mishap. They breathed sighs of relief when I said I was just a pilot.

After my time in Helena, I decided to rent a car to drive back to Billings instead of gambling by flying on Big Sky Airlines again.

Big Sky Airlines ceased operations in 2008.

CHAPTER 15

THE VIRUS

The Portland, Oregon, airport has been named the best airport in the United States year after year. It is one of my favorite airports, and I always try to get to PDX, as it is known, early when I am flying from there. The shops, restaurants, and spectacular views make it a destination not to be missed, and I enjoy walking through the terminals and reflecting on the beauty of the airport and surrounding area.

While writing this book, I had an extra three hours at PDX due to a delayed flight to Denver, so I decided to go to the farthest, most secluded part of terminal E to find a quiet place to write. I wasn't looking for a remote area just for silence; I also was trying to stay as far away as possible from other people. A new virus was making its way through the world: a novel coronavirus that caused a disease called COVID-19. News of the virus was on every TV in the airport terminal, as well as on my cell phone and everyone else's at PDX.

To my delight, there were no passengers or any other humans in the area of gate E11, so I took up space near the windows for a view of the north runway.

I put on my headphones to drown out any distractions, plugged them into my laptop, and began typing. The driving rhythm of the Reverend Horton Heat songs I was listening to put me into a groove as thoughts became words, and I typed in double time along with the music.

An Alaska Airlines Boeing 737 was rotating to the sky as I looked up from my computer to see where the sound of someone coughing was coming from. I looked to my right, and the waiting area was still empty of people in that direction. I then looked to my left as another cough came out of the mouth of a guy who had decided to sit directly behind me. For some reason, he had taken that particular seat despite the hundreds of other open seats in the area. He wasn't alone, and a man who looked like his twin brother began coughing in my direction. In unison, the two pulled up the medical masks around their necks to cover their faces. They completed the task by pulling the elastic straps of the masks over their ears and began to speak to each other in Chinese.

As I closed my laptop in frustration and placed my computer in my backpack, the twins continually coughed.

Why would these guys sit in those seats, with all the other open seats in the gate area? I thought to myself as I gathered my belongings and walked away.

I walked to gate E3, from which the flight to Denver would leave an hour later. It looked to be a full flight, as passengers occupied every seat in the waiting area. As I leaned against a column near the gate area, I watched a news report blast on a TV that hung over the waiting passengers. News of Italy shutting down towns due to the virus was headlined, and a news ticker at the bottom of the screen announced a growing number of patients with the virus in nearby Seattle.

My cell phone rang as I continued to watch the news-ticker updates, which heightened my hopes that the coughing twins would not be on the same flight.

"It's your brother. When are you home?" my brother, Paul, asked.

"I'm at the gate, about to board the flight to Denver," I replied.

"What are you doing next week?" Paul asked. "I need your help in Phoenix."

"For what?" I said.

"Have you been watching the news? This virus thing is getting real, and I need to pick up some stuff in Peoria to make hand sanitizer."

"Hand sanitizer?" I asked.

"Yeah, a guy closed down his distillery, and I need to get bottles and some product to help our distillery in Denver make sanitizer. All the distilleries are making it. It's going to get crazy," said Paul.

"I'll call you when I get on the ground in Denver. Gotta board the plane now," I said as the gate agent announced group-one boarding.

"Make sure you do. I really need your help," he said.

I hung up the phone and boarded the flight, wondering what possible opportunity there might be in making hand sanitizer. As I took my seat, a cough from a boarding passenger made me think about the rapidly changing world in the face of the coronavirus. Maybe my brother was onto something.

Ten days later, my brother and I were at Denver International Airport to take an early-morning one-way flight to Phoenix, Arizona. Flights from Europe to the United States had been banned that morning after the World Health Organization declared the coronavirus a pandemic. It was obvious people were taking the virus seriously, as the airport was like a ghost town, and the usual lines of passengers were nonexistent as we made our way to the security checkpoint.

My brother and I passed through security and made it to the gate for our flight to Phoenix in record time. Only a handful of passengers were in the waiting area for the quick flight to Arizona, and thanks to the light load, Paul and I were upgraded to row one, seats A and B, in first class.

After a quick boarding process, the main cabin door closed earlier than usual. As the safety briefing was about to begin, I asked the flight attendant how many passengers were on the flight. She responded that a total of just twenty-nine passengers were on board, the least amount of passengers she had ever seen in more than thirty years of being a flight attendant.

Soon we were taxiing to the departure runway, when my brother nudged me in the arm.

"Look at that guy," he said, looking toward the passenger in seat 1D.

A middle-aged male passenger sitting in seat 1D was wearing khaki shorts and a pink polo shirt. He had leaned back in his seat and put both of his feet up high on the fabric partition that divided the first-class passengers from the service galley. The passenger sitting next to the guy's V-shaped body looked horrified as the plane readied for takeoff.

The passenger in 1D was looking at his cell phone, when a flight attendant doing a final check told him to take his ratty blue tennis shoes off the partition and place his feet on the floor. He complied but put one of his feet back up on the partition the minute the flight attendant took her seat for takeoff. His leg remained in the air during takeoff and the climb out and for most of the hour-and-twenty-minute flight.

The flight to Phoenix was uneventful and eerily quiet, even after we touched down at Sky Harbor International Airport. The normal bustling sound of travelers preparing to get off the plane was missing as the Boeing stopped at the arrival gate. But my brother and I were on a mission and quickly deplaned so we could meet our sister, Rae, for a ride to a Penske truck rental facility in West Phoenix.

Terminal 2 at Sky Harbor International was empty of passengers, just as we had seen in Denver. It was surreal to see, and the possibility of not getting back to Colorado was beginning to sink in.

"We have to hustle," said Paul. "Sis is picking us up, and we need to get to the truck rental. They are closing at noon."

Paul's plan was to pick up a rental truck, load it up with the supplies at the distillery, have a good dinner with the owner, and then start back to Colorado. However, that all changed when restaurants were ordered to close to the public that morning and could only offer food for takeout or delivery. We decided to load up the truck and drive to Albuquerque, New Mexico, in time to grab a takeout steak dinner from one of my brother's favorite places, which was next to a hotel he wanted to stay at that night.

We walked to the south side of terminal 2, where we met our sister, who was wearing a face mask and rubber gloves.

"It's getting bad down here. All kinds of places are shutting down," she said as we loaded our bags into her car and then got in the car and drove out of the airport.

"We gotta get to a Home Depot for supplies and pick up the truck quick," replied my brother as he texted the owner of the distillery.

"Home Depot is on the way and should be open," my sister said as we got onto westbound Interstate 10.

"Any luck with the owner?" I asked Paul as he continued texting.

"Nothing," said Paul. "He will be there."

I looked at my watch and figured that if all went well with our getting the truck loaded and getting on the road, Paul and I could make it to Albuquerque by eight o'clock that night.

After we made a quick stop at Home Depot for packing supplies, our sister dropped us off at a storage facility that was supposed to have a twenty-foot truck ready for pickup. The gates were locked in front of the office, and there were no trucks in sight.

"Now what?" I asked Paul as he was about to dial the storage facility on his cell phone.

Just as Paul placed his cell phone to his ear, a door cracked open from the storage office.

"Can I help you?" said a lady's voice through the narrow opening.

"We have a truck rented," said Paul.

"Just put your license and credit card on the ground through the gate, and step back," said the lady.

Paul looked at me in disgust, pulled out the items from his wallet, and placed them on the ground through the locked gate. He stepped back away from the gate, and an older lady opened the door, slowly walked out of the office, and picked up the items.

"I'll be right back," she said, and she turned to a younger lady and told her to go get a truck. The sound of a door opening and then slamming closed came from the back of the office.

A few minutes later, the older lady returned to the gate with a clipboard with rental documents and Paul's license and credit card attached.

"It's the virus, you know," said the lady as she slid the clipboard under the gate. "Truck is coming around," she added as the sound of a diesel truck fired up in the back of the storage facility.

Paul reviewed the documents and scribbled his name on the bottom of them as a massive twenty-six-foot box truck pulled up to the office. The sound of an air brake hissed as the engine was shut down.

"We had a twenty-foot truck reserved," Paul told the old lady.

"This is all we've got. It's the virus, you know. Same rate," said the old lady through the gate as the younger lady cautiously handed the keys to my brother.

"Have a safe trip," said the younger lady as she quickly walked to the gate, which the older lady had opened.

"Well, this ought to be fun," I said to myself, thinking about possible crosswinds on I-25 from Albuquerque to Denver due to a winter storm moving through the area.

The huge truck might as well have been a giant sail that could easily be tipped over onto its side, just as many semitrucks had been blown over in the past on I-25. But because of the tight time frame and uncertainty in the world, we got in the truck and headed toward the distillery. We had an hour to load up and get on the road to make it to Albuquerque by eight o'clock.

"Any word from the owner of the distillery?" I asked my brother as we pulled out of the storage facility.

"Nothing, but he will be there," Paul said. "We are only ten minutes from the distillery. Should be a quick load."

Three hours later, the supplies that should have taken just an hour to load were firmly strapped down in the rental truck. Hundreds of empty bottles, corks, other supplies, and a heavy metal pallet rack, which we had to take apart, filled up just half of the box truck. Physically exhausted, my brother and I said our goodbyes to the owner of the distillery and began the drive to New Mexico.

As my brother drove the truck on the 101 loop around the west side of Phoenix, I got a text message from my wife saying that more than a foot of snow had fallen in the Denver area that morning. She was glad we were spending the night in Albuquerque and not driving straight through. She also texted that businesses were shutting down, along with schools, but the biggest news was the dramatic fall in the stock market. Only a few weeks earlier, the stock market had been at an all-time high, but fear of the coronavirus had the market in a free fall.

For the next six hours, I monitored the news and the stock market as Paul drove the giant truck toward Albuquerque. Auto traffic was unusually light on the highway, but the many semitrucks seemed to be moving their loads on time. The normally packed casinos along the route had empty parking lots, and their neon signs announced that they were closed until further notice. This was a road trip unlike any I had ever experienced.

Night had fallen as we neared Grants, New Mexico, just an hour outside Albuquerque. We pulled into a truck stop for fuel, and I tried to open the passenger door to get out to use the bathroom. Nothing happened. I tried pulling the door handle harder to see if it would release the latch, but again, nothing happened. I verified that the door lock was not engaged and tried again to no avail. My only option was to climb over to the driver's side of the truck cab and exit out of the driver's-side door. Paul got out of the truck, and I followed him into the convenience store.

As I went to use the men's room, Paul walked around the store, looking for some chips to munch on over the next hour of driving. After a quick pee and a good hand washing, I rejoined Paul in the store as he walked up to pay for a bag of chips in his hand. The cashiers were standing behind a security wall made of clear plastic when my brother walked up to pay for the chips.

"We're on lockdown," said a female cashier behind the plastic. "Can't take your money."

"Why?" asked my brother.

"One of the truckers thinks he has the virus," she answered as a guy in a yellow vest began to spray something onto the entry door we had just walked through.

My brother, with a look of horror on his face, carefully put the bag of chips back on the rack he had taken them from. "Let's get out of here," he said to me. "Why the hell didn't they tell us that when we came in?" he added as we walked out the door.

I climbed back into the truck through the driver's-side door and over to the passenger seat, and my brother quickly followed. He started the engine and headed out of the truck stop. Across the parking lot, we could see the flashing lights of an ambulance and a police car next to a semitruck, one of dozens of trucks parked for the night.

"Why wouldn't they have said anything?" said my brother again as he pulled the truck back onto Interstate 40. I could see concern on his face for the rest of the drive.

We got to Albuquerque around ten o'clock. No restaurants were open upon our arrival, and to add insult to injury, the beer cooler at the hotel we stayed at was locked up at nine o'clock by law. It was a long day, followed by a short night.

The snowstorm that had dumped a foot of fresh powder in Colorado had moved to the east when we began the seven-hour drive from New Mexico to Denver the next morning.

Continued news of the stock market free fall and the coronavirus's effects around the world kept coming in as we drove north on I-25. As predicted, the wind out of the west blew against the truck, and we saw several blown-over semitrucks sitting helplessly in the median of the highway as we worked our way to Colorado.

Fortunately, the weather and traffic worked in our favor, and we arrived safely in Denver at four o'clock that afternoon, just as the governor of Colorado announced the closure of all nonessential businesses for the next forty-five days. Five days later, the governor put the State of Colorado in complete lockdown with a stay-at-home order.

COVID-19 had changed the world.

Distilleries were declared essential businesses during the pandemic. I helped my brother make a thousand gallons of hand sanitizer and personally delivered nearly one hundred gallons, which were donated to local police and fire departments, along with a hospital in Boulder, Colorado.

Who would have ever guessed that distilleries would go from making whiskey to making hand sanitizer?

All because of a virus.

Special thanks go out to all the first responders and medical personnel who worked unbelievably hard hours during the pandemic.

You are all heroes.

EPILOGUE

A five-year-old boy stood holding a pair of drumsticks near gate B11 at Denver International Airport. He was joined by his mom and dad for the flight to Orlando, Florida, which was scheduled to leave in forty-five minutes.

"Son, you have some time—get busy!" the dad said to his son.

The five-year-old held the drumsticks out in front of him and walked over to an empty chair in the waiting area. He began to beat the drumsticks as he counted out loud.

"Paradiddle, paradiddle, paradiddle," said the boy as he beat the chair.

"You're doing good, Son!" said the dad with a smile on his face. "You're gonna win!"

"Paradiddle, paradiddle," said the boy as passengers lined up for the flight.

A guy in front of me turned around and said, "God, I hope that kid isn't next to me. Can't stand little kids."

I didn't respond to the comment but watched how the kid changed his drumming pattern and continued to practice with good rhythm.

He is a really good drummer, I thought as the boarding process began.

The little drummer's dad said, "Okay, Son, let's go win a competition."

The kid stopped drumming and stuffed his sticks into the back pocket of his little Levi's.

"God, I hate kids," said the guy in front of me again.

I thought to myself, *We're going to Orlando, man! Families with kids are everywhere. What do you expect?*

I settled into my window seat, 11A, for the flight to Orlando, and I noticed the guy who didn't like kids was sitting in seat 12A behind me. The two seats next to him were empty, and I thought nothing would be better than for the little drummer boy to sit next to him on the flight.

The little drummer boy's family got on the plane near the end of the boarding process, and seats 12B and 12C were still empty as they got closer to row twelve. At the last minute, a guy ahead of the drummer boy's family took seat 12C on the aisle.

I heard the guy behind me say, "Thank God that didn't happen."

Immediately afterward, the little drummer boy took seat 13A behind the guy. The cabin door closed, and as the plane was about to push back from the gate, I heard the kid's dad say, "Get busy, Son! We've got a competition."

You just never know what you will see on an airline flight.

AIRLINE ETIQUETTE

- Don't hold up boarding.
- Remember that your backpack can cause injuries.
- Put down your phone to listen to the safety briefing.
- Don't stink, and admit if it's your own fart.
- Don't take your shoes off if your feet stink or are gross.
- If your kid is acting up, remember, you're the parent.
- Take dirty diapers and other trash with you when you exit the plane.
- Keep your swearing to yourself.
- Pay attention to what your pet is doing.
- Don't flip your hair over the headrest.
- Share the armrests.
- Use your inside voice when talking.
- Don't grab on to the seat in front of you to pull yourself up.
- Be nice to the flight attendants and crew.
- Just be nice.

APPENDIX

AIRCRAFT FEATURED IN *SEAT 29B*

The Douglas DC-4A/C-54 Skymaster

When it was decided that the president of the United States, Franklin D. Roosevelt, should have a personal airplane to transport him to meetings around the world, the aircraft of choice was the US Army Air Corps' C-54A Skymaster. Dubbed the Sacred Cow, the plane took the president to Tehran, Casablanca, Hawaii, and other less exotic spots in the United States.

The C-54 was the military derivative of the Douglas DC-4, a four-engine long-range airliner with a three-man crew and accommodations for up to forty-nine passengers or twenty-six troops. Originally designed to a specification from United Airlines, the DC-4 had a maximum speed of 274 miles per hour and a range of 3,900 miles. The first sixty-one civilian orders were followed by seventy-one more from the US Army Air Corps, though in the end, most ended up in army service.

To meet the military's more stringent needs, the DC-4 was given a cargo door, a stronger floor, a cargo boom hoist, and larger wing tanks. The first flight of the military C-54 occurred on March 26, 1942. During the war years, 1,242 C-54s were delivered with a wide variety of modifications. A few of the major ones were the C-54A, the original fully militarized model capable of lifting fifty soldiers or 32,500 pounds of cargo; the JC-54D, which was modified for missile nose cone recovery; the C-54E, with larger Pratt and Whitney engines, bigger fuel tanks for longer range, and a specially designed cabin for quick conversion between passenger and cargo roles; the C-54M, which was a C-54E stripped out to serve as a coal carrier during the Berlin Airlift; the EC-54U, a postwar modification as an electronic countermeasures platform; and at least fourteen subvariants built for the US Navy originally called the R5D. There were numerous other variants that performed countless other roles, from VIP transport to multiengine training.

The C-54 offered sterling service for both the USAF and the US Navy after the war and was not fully retired until the late 1960s. Ex-military Skymasters became popular as cargo transports and fire bombers, and many are still in active use around the world in these roles. A lucky few have been acquired by appreciative warbird groups in the United States.

Nicknames
- The Sacred Cow (FDR's personal transport)
- Rescuemaster (US Air Force's SC-54D air-sea rescue variant)

Specifications
- Engines: Four 1,450-horsepower Pratt and Whitney R-2000-2SD-13G Twin Wasp radial piston engines
- Weight:
  - Empty: 43,300 pounds
  - Maximum takeoff: 73,000 pounds
- Wing span: 117 feet, 6 inches
- Length: 93 feet, 10 inches
- Height: 27 feet, 6 inches

Performance
- Maximum speed: 280 miles per hour at 14,000 feet
- Ceiling: 22,300 feet
- Range: 2,500 miles
- Armament: None

Number built
- 1,000-plus (military versions)

Number still airworthy
- At least 100

The Consolidated PBY Catalina

From its introduction to US naval service in 1936, through its continued international military use into the 1970s, to the recent retirement of the last civilian firebomber, the Consolidated PBY Catalina has served a distinguished career as one of the most rugged and versatile aircraft in US history. It was created in response to the US Navy's 1933 request for a prototype to replace the Consolidated P2Y and the Martin P3M with a new patrol-bomber flying boat with extended range and greater load capacity.

The Catalina was created under the guidance of the brilliant aeroengineer Isaac Macklin Laddon. The new design introduced internal wing bracing, which greatly reduced the need for drag-producing struts and bracing wires. A significant improvement over its predecessors, it had a range of 2,545 miles and a maximum takeoff weight of 35,420 pounds. In 1939, the navy considered discontinuing its use in favor of proposed replacements. The Catalina remained in production, however, because of massive orders placed by Britain, Canada, Australia, France, and the Netherlands. These countries desperately needed reliable patrol planes in their eleventh-hour preparations for World War II. Far from replacing the PBY, the navy placed its largest single order since World War I for an aircraft.

Over the years, numerous improvements were made to the design, and many variants were produced under license by several different companies.

An amphibious version, the PBY-5A, was developed in 1939 through the addition of a retractable tricycle undercarriage. The PBY-6A featured hydrodynamic improvements designed by the Naval Aircraft Factory. The Soviet Union produced a license-built version for their navy called the GST and powered by Mikulin M-62 radial engines. Boeing Aircraft of Canada built the PB2B-1 and PB2B-2 (Canso), and a derivative of the PBY-5A called the PBV-1A was built by Canadian Vickers. In US Army Air Force service, the aircraft was known as the OA-10A (PBY-5A) and OA-10B (PBY-6A). The Royal Air Force's Coastal Command flew Catalinas under the designations Catalina Mk I, II, III, and IV. The Naval Aircraft Factory built a similar-looking version called the PBN-1 Nomad, which can rightly be called a different aircraft, as the changes were so extensive.

A total of approximately four thousand Catalinas and variants were built between 1936 and 1945. Because of their worldwide popularity, there was scarcely a maritime battle in World War II in which they were not involved.

The PBY had its vulnerabilities: it was slow, with a maximum speed of 179 miles per hour, and with no crew armor or self-sealing tanks, it was highly vulnerable to antiaircraft attack. However, it was those weaknesses, coincident with the development of effective radar and Japanese reliance on night transport, that led to the development of the Black Cat squadrons. These crews performed nighttime search and attack missions in their black-painted PBYs. The tactics were spectacularly successful and seriously disrupted the flow of supplies and personnel to Japanese island bases. The Catalinas also proved effective in search and rescue missions, code-named Dumbo. Small detachments, normally of three PBYs, routinely orbited on standby near targeted combat areas. One detachment based in the Solomon Islands rescued 161 airmen between January 1 and August 15, 1943, and successes increased steadily as equipment and tactics improved. After World War II, the PBY continued its search and rescue service in many Central and South American countries, as well as in Denmark, until the 1970s.

The Catalina also proved useful in civilian service—in scheduled passenger flights in Alaska and the Caribbean, in geophysical survey, and, mostly, in firebombing for the US Forest Service—until the retirement of the last PBY in the early 1980s. Through its long and varied service, the

Consolidated PBY Catalina and its numerous variants have earned their reputation as workhorses of naval aviation.

Nicknames
- Cat
- Mad Cat (when outfitted with magnetic anomaly detection gear)
- Black Cat (night variant)
- Pig Boat
- P-Boat
- Y-Boat (Dutch navy nickname)
- Canso or Canso A (Canadian designation)
- Mop (NATO designation for Soviet lend-lease PBYs)

Specifications (PBY-5A)
- Engines: Two 1,200-horsepower Pratt and Whitney R-1830-92 Twin Wasp radial piston engines
- Weight:
  - Empty: 20,910 pounds
  - Maximum takeoff: 35,420 pounds
- Wing span: 104 feet, 0 inches
- Length: 63 feet, 10.5 inches
- Height: 20 feet, 2 inches

Performance
- Maximum speed: 179 miles per hour
- Long-range cruising speed: 117 miles per hour
- Ceiling: 14,700 feet
- Range: 2,545 miles
- Armament:
  - Five 7.62-millimeter (0.3-inch) machine guns
  - Up to 4,000 pounds of bombs or depth charges

Number built
- Approximately 4,000

Number still airworthy
- Approximately 30

The Mitsubishi A6M Zero

Fast, maneuverable, and flown by highly skilled pilots, the Mitsubishi Zero-Sen was the most famous Japanese plane of World War II and a big surprise to American forces. Ignored by British and American intelligence services, who had access to design plans for the aircraft years before the war, the Zero—the navy's Type 0 carrier-based fighter—was armed with two 20-millimeter cannons and two 7.7-millimeter machine guns and possessed the incredible range of 1,930 miles using a centerline drop tank. Though outclassed by more powerful US fighters after late 1943, the Zero remained a tough opponent throughout the war.

First flown on April 1, 1939, the A6M1 prototype was powered by a 780-horsepower Mitsubishi Zuisei radial engine, which gave it excellent performance, except for its maximum speed, which was below navy specifications. A second prototype, the A6M2, was powered by a 925-horsepower Nakajima Sakae engine, which was so successful that in July 1940, the type was ordered into production as the navy's Type 0 carrier-fighter model 11. Other variants were rapidly introduced, including a two-seat trainer, the A6M2-K; a Nakajima-built floatplane version called the A6M2-N; a performance-increased version called the A6M5; and several reengined versions late in the war, which culminated in the 1,130-horsepower A6M8.

Preproduction Zeros were used in China from August 1940. This outstanding aircraft could travel at speeds up to 350 miles per hour in level flight (the A6M5 version) and reach 15,000 feet in five minutes. America's front-line fighter, the Grumman F4F Wildcat, had a top speed of 325 miles per hour; was not as maneuverable; and had four .50-inch machine guns. No wonder the few Wildcat pilots rising up to defend Pearl Harbor in December 1941 were surprised!

By late 1944, with most of its aircraft carriers sunk and its most highly trained aircrews gone, Japan resorted to desperate measures. These included kamikaze (divine wind) suicide raids, wherein green pilots turned their early model Zeros into aerial bombs for attacks on Allied ships during the battles of Okinawa, Iwo Jima, and the Philippines. Truly an ignominious end for one of history's great warbirds.

Only five Zeros are considered to be airworthy today (and only one with its original Sakae engine), making them among the rarest and most prized warbirds on the display circuit today.

Nicknames
- Reisen (*Rei Shiko Sentoki*, Japanese for "Type 0 Fighter")
- Zeke (Allied reporting name)
- Zero

Specifications (A6M5)
- Engine: One 1,130-horsepower Nakajima NK1C Sakae 21 radial piston engine
- Weight:
  o Empty: 4,175 pounds
  o Maximum takeoff: 6,504 pounds
- Wing span: 36 feet, 1inch
- Length: 29 feet, 9 inches
- Height: 11 feet, 5.75 inches

Performance
- Maximum speed: 346 miles per hour
- Ceiling: 35,100 feet
- Range: 1,118 miles with internal fuel
- Armament:
  o Two 20-millimeter cannons
  o Two 7.7-millimeter machine guns

Number built
- 10,500

Number still airworthy
- Five

The Messerschmitt Bf 109

In the mid-1930s, the Luftwaffe began to modernize its fighter aircraft fleet. A competition for new designs was held, resulting in at least four competitors. Two designs were selected for further development, one being Willy Messerschmitt's Bf 109, a single-seat derivation of his previously successful Bf 108 design. The first 109 prototype, powered by a 695-horsepower Rolls-Royce Kestrel engine, first flew on May 28, 1935. The second prototype was fitted with the engine for which it had been designed, the 610-horsepower Junkers Jumo 210A. Preproduction prototypes had various combinations of armament and engines.

The first production model, the Bf 109B-1, was delivered in early 1937 to the JG132 Richthofen squadron, Germany's top fighter unit. The new fighters quickly established a good combat reputation in the Spanish Civil War later that year. The next production variant, the Bf 109C-1, appeared in the fall of 1937 and utilized a more powerful 700-horsepower Jumo 210Ga engine. Demand for the airplane was so great that it was built under license by no fewer than four other companies, including Arado, Erla, Focke-Wulf, and Fieseler.

By the time World War II began in 1939, the Luftwaffe had more than one thousand Bf 109s in service, and the aircraft was to play a major role in all further fighter operations. Allied bombing gradually slowed German aircraft production, but 109s were also built by WNF in Austria and in Hungary. During and after the war, Messerschmitt exported thousands of Bf 109s to Bulgaria, Finland, Hungary, Japan, Romania, Slovakia, Spain, Switzerland, the USSR, and Yugoslavia. In addition, the Spanish company Hispano produced the Bf 109 under license beginning in 1945, calling it the HA-1109. Their HA-1110 and HA-1112 variants were a two-seater and a modified single-seater, respectively. Several engines were fitted, including the 1,300-horsepower Hispano-Suiza HS-12Z-89 and the 1,400-horsepower Rolls-Royce Merlin 500-45.

Yet another source of Bf 109 production was Czechoslovakia, where the company Avia supplied S-99 and S-199 variants, many of which remained in service until 1957.

Total production is estimated at thirty-five thousand, making it one of the most numerous aircraft types of the war.

Nicknames
- Augsburg Eagle
- Buchon Pounter Pigeon (HA-1112)
- Mezec Mule (Avia S-199)
- Anton (A-Model)
- Bertha (B-Model)
- Clara (C-Model)
- Dora (D-Model)
- Emil (E-Model)
- Fritz (F-Model)
- Gustav (G-Model)
- Beule or Bump (Bf 109G-1 Trop)
- Toni (T-Model)

Specifications (Bf 109G-6)
- Engine: 1,800-horsepower Daimler-Benz DB-605 inverted V-12 piston engine
- Weight:
  o Empty: 5,893 pounds
  o Maximum takeoff: 6,945 pounds
- Wing span: 32 feet, 6.5 inches
- Length: 29 feet, 7 inches
- Height: 11 feet, 2 inches

Performance
- Maximum speed at 23,000 feet: 385 miles per hour
- Ceiling: 38,500 feet
- Range: 450 miles
- Armament:
    o Two 13-millimeter (0.51-inch) MG131 machine guns
    o Three 20-millimeter MG151 cannons

Number built
- Approximately 35,000

Number still airworthy
- Approximately 10 (and approximately two-thirds are HA-112s)

The Supermarine Spitfire

Undoubtedly the most famous British combat aircraft of World War II, the Spitfire is as deeply ingrained in the collective psyche of most Britons as the P-51 Mustang is in most Americans'. First flown on March 5, 1936, the Spitfire sprang from the design desk of R. J. Mitchell, who had previously submitted an unsuccessful design for a similar fighter, the Type 224. Once he was given the freedom to design an aircraft outside of the strict Air Ministry specifications, his Type 300 emerged as a clear winner—so much so that a new Air Ministry specification was written to match the new design.

The Spitfire Mk I became operational at Duxford, Cambridgeshire, in July 1938, and as time went on, the Spitfire became one of the most versatile and most modified aircraft in existence, with various wing designs, armament changes, and engine changes dictating its many identities.

By the time World War II began in September 1939, nine squadrons of Spits were operational with the RAF, and the Spitfire quickly lived up to its good reputation by downing a German He 111 over the United Kingdom the following month. Ten more Spitfire squadrons were on strength by the fall of 1940, when the Battle of Britain tested the nation's resolve and military resources. Spitfires soon began overseas operations in Malta, the Middle East, and the Pacific.

The Spitfire served, and continued to be built, throughout World War

II. It served in many theaters and with many Allied nations, including the United States and the Soviet Union.

The Royal Navy, noting both the success of the Spitfire in land-based service and the success of their own Sea Hurricanes, ordered the production of the Seafire, a carrier-based version of the Spitfire. Deliveries began in January 1942, and the Seafire was used in growing numbers and variants throughout the remainder of the war.

While certainly not all-inclusive or comprehensive, this list of some of the most significant variants of the Spitfire and Seafire give some idea of the complexity of the aircraft's history:

- Mk IB: Four 7.7-millimeter (0.303-inch) guns and two 20-millimeter cannons
- Mk VA, B, and C: More powerful Merlin engine, provisions for drop tanks or bombs, wing and armament changes
- Mk VII: High-altitude interceptor with pressurized cockpit and retractable tailwheel
- Mk VIII: Pure fighter with unpressurized cockpit
- Mk IX: Two-stage Merlin engine mated to Mk V airframe
- Mk XIV: Griffon 65/66 engine with five-bladed propeller, strengthened fuselage, broad tail (late models had a bubble canopy)
- Mk XVI: Packard Merlin engine (many had a bubble canopy)
- Seafire Mk IIC: Catapult hooks and strengthened landing gear, Merlin engine, four-blade propeller
- Seafire Mk III: Double folding wings and 1,585-horsepower Merlin 55 engine

The last operational mission of the Spitfire took place on April 1, 1954, when a Spitfire PR Mk XIX flew a photo-reconnaissance mission over Malaya. The final mission of the Seafire was in 1967, after many years of faithful service with the Fleet Air Arm and various training squadrons.

The Spitfire, one of the most significant and revered fighter aircraft ever built, continues to steal the lion's share of attention at airshows and fly-ins. The remaining examples are flown with great care, and continued Spitfire restorations ensure that this beautiful aircraft will continue to delight pilots and spectators alike for the foreseeable future.

Nicknames
- Spit
- Spitter
- Bomfire (Spitfires used as fighter-bombers)

Specifications (Mk VA)
- Engine: One 1,478-horsepower Rolls-Royce Merlin 45 V-12 piston engine
- Weight:
  o Empty: 4,998 pounds
  o Maximum takeoff: 6,417 pounds
- Wing span: 36 feet, 10 inches
- Length: 29 feet, 11 inches
- Height: 9 feet, 11 inches

Performance
- Maximum speed: 369 miles per hour
- Ceiling: 36,500 feet
- Range: 1,135 miles
- Armament:
  o Eight 7.7-millimeter (0.303-inch) Browning machine guns
  o Other variants carried either two cannons and four machine guns; four cannons; or two cannons, two 12.7-millimeter machine guns, and 1,000 pounds of bombs

Number built
- 20,334 Spitfires
- 2,556 Seafires

Number still airworthy
- Approximately 55

The North American P-51 Mustang

One of the most effective, famous, and beautiful fighter aircraft of World War II, the P-51, was designed to fulfill a British requirement dated April 1940. Because of the rapidly mounting clouds of war in Europe, the United Kingdom asked North American Aircraft to design and build a new fighter in only 120 days. The NA-73X prototype was produced in record time, but it did not fly until October 26, 1940. The first RAF production models, designated Mustang Mk Is, underwent rigorous testing and evaluation, and it was found that the 1,100-horsepower Allison engine was well suited for low-altitude tactical reconnaissance, but the engine's power decreased dramatically above an altitude of twelve thousand feet, making it a poor choice for air-to-air combat or interception roles. Because of this, the RAF left its eight machine guns intact but also fitted the Mustang with cameras. In this configuration, it served in at least twenty-three RAF squadrons, beginning in April 1942.

At the same time, the US Army Air Corps ordered a small number for tactical reconnaissance evaluation as the F-6A. After the RAF found the aircraft's performance lacking, they tested a new engine, the twelve-cylinder Rolls-Royce Merlin. This gave much-improved performance and led to the USAAF fitting two airframes with 1,430-horsepower Packard-built Merlin V-1650 engines. These aircraft were redesignated XP-51B. Practically overnight, the aircraft's potential began to grow.

Since the RAF had had good success with the Mustang in a ground attack role, the USAAF bought five hundred aircraft fitted with dive brakes and underwing weapons pylons. These were initially designated the A-36A Apache but later retained the name Mustang. Almost simultaneously, they ordered 310 P-51As with Allison engines. Some of these were delivered to the United Kingdom as Mustang Mk IIs, and some became F-6B reconnaissance aircraft for the USAAF.

The first Merlin-engine versions appeared in 1943 with the P-51B, of which 1,988 were built in Inglewood, California, and the P-51C, of which 1,750 were built in Dallas, Texas. Both new versions had strengthened fuselages and four wing-mounted 12.7-millimeter machine guns. Many of these new Mustangs were delivered to the United Kingdom as Mustang Mk IIIs, and others went to the USAAF as F-6Cs. The Merlin-powered Mustangs were exactly what the Allied bombers in Europe desperately needed, and they became famous for their long range and potent high-altitude escort capability. The most significant variant, the P-51D, featured a 360-degree-view bubble canopy, a modified rear fuselage, and six 12.77-millimeter machine guns. The number built was 7,956, and once again, many went to the United Kingdom as Mustang Mk IVs, and others became USAAF F-6D reconnaissance aircraft. Next came the P-51K, which was generally similar. A third of these became RAF Mustang IVs also, and more than a hundred became F-6Ks. Very late in the war, the P-51H appeared, although only 555 of 2,000 were completed before V-J Day caused the cancellation of the order. US production totaled 15,386, but at least 200 more were built by the Commonwealth Aircraft Corporation of Australia with imported parts and designated Mustang Mk 20, 21, 22, and 23. None of these saw service before the end of the war. Under the lend-lease program, fifty P-51s were supplied to China, and forty more were supplied to the Netherlands in the Pacific theater.

After the war, the P-51 remained in US service with the Strategic Air Command until 1949 and with the Air National Guard and Reserves into the 1950s. It became one of the first fighters to see combat in the Korean War. The RAF's Fighter Command used them until 1946. In addition, more than fifty air forces around the world acquired and used the Mustang for many more years, some as recently as the early 1980s. When the US Air Force realigned their aircraft designations in the 1950s, the Mustang became the F-51.

In the last forty years, surplus Mustangs have been modified and used extensively as civilian air racers, but the latest trend is for private owners to restore them to almost perfect, historically accurate condition. As public appreciation for the Mustang has grown, the monetary value of the few remaining examples has skyrocketed. War-surplus P-51s, once auctioned from storage for less than US $2,000, are now usually valued at nearly a million dollars or more. The restoration of existing airframes has become a small industry in the United States, the United Kingdom, and Australia, and the total number of flyable examples, despite one or two accidents each year, is growing. Several Mustangs have been or are currently being restored as two-seat, dual-control TF-51s, a trend that promises to ensure that today's operators are better trained than any previous generation of Mustang pilots.

Nicknames
- Fifty-One
- 'Stang
- Peter Dash Flash

Specifications (P-51D)
- Engine: One 1,695-horsepower Packard Merlin V-1650-7 piston V-12 engine
- Weight:
  o Empty: 7,125 pounds
  o Maximum takeoff: 12,100 pounds
- Wing span: 37 feet, 0.5 inches
- Length: 32 feet, 9.5 inches
- Height: 13 feet, 8 inches

Performance
- Maximum speed: 437 miles per hour
- Ceiling: 41,900 feet
- Range: 1,300 miles
- Armament: Six 12.7-millimeter (0.5-inch) wing-mounted machine guns, plus up to two 1,000-pound bombs or six 127-millimeter (5-inch) rockets

Number built
- Approximately 15,018 (including approximately 200 built in Australia)

Number still airworthy
- Approximately 150

Number of flyable P-82 Twin Mustangs
- Two

The Grumman OV-1 Mohawk

The Grumman OV-1 Mohawk began as a joint US Army-Marine program through the then Navy Bureau of Aeronautics (BuAer) for an observation and attack plane that would outperform the Cessna L-19 Bird Dog. In June 1956, the army issued Type Specification TS145, which called for the development and procurement of a two-seat twin turboprop aircraft designed to operate from small, unimproved fields under all weather conditions. It would be faster and have greater firepower and heavier armor than the Bird Dog, which had proven vulnerable during the Korean War. The Mohawk's mission would include observation, artillery spotting, air control, emergency resupply, naval target spotting, liaison, and radiological monitoring. The navy specified that the aircraft must be capable of operating from small jeep escort carriers (CVEs). The Department of Defense selected Grumman Aircraft Corporation's G-134 design as the winner of the competition in 1957. Marine requirements contributed an unusual feature to the design. As originally proposed, the OF-1 could be fitted with water skis that would allow the aircraft to land at sea and taxi to island beaches at twenty knots. Since the marines were authorized to operate fixed-wing aircraft in the close air support (CAS) role, the mock-up also featured underwing pylons for rockets, bombs, and other stores.

The radar imaging capability of the Mohawk proved a significant advance in both peace and war. The side-looking airborne radar (SLAR) could look through foliage and map terrain, presenting the observer with a film image of the earth below only minutes after the area was scanned. In military operations, the image was split into two parts, with one showing fixed terrain features and the other spotting moving targets.

The prototype (YAO-1AF) first flew on April 14, 1959. The OV-1 entered production in October 1959.

As of 2011, Alliant Techsystems partnered with the Broadbay Group and Mohawk Technologies of Florida in a venture to return an armed, modernized version of the OV-1D to operational use as a counterinsurgency aircraft. A demonstrator was equipped with a FLIR Star SAFIRE turret and a trainable ventral M230 chain gun.

General characteristics
- Crew: Two (pilot and observer)
- Length: 41 feet, 0 inches
- Wing span: 48 feet, 0 inches
- Height: 12 feet, 8 inches
- Wing area: 360 square feet
- Empty weight: 12,054 pounds
- Loaded weight: 15,544 pounds (normal takeoff weight for IR mission)
- Maximum takeoff weight: 18,109 pounds (SLAR mission)
- Power plant: Two Lycoming T53-L-701 turboprops with 1,400 shaft horsepower each

Performance
- Never-exceed speed: 450 miles per hour (390 knots)
- Maximum speed: 305 miles per hour (265 knots) at 10,000 feet (IR mission)
- Cruise speed: 207 miles per hour (180 knots, econ cruise)
- Stall speed: 84 miles per hour (73 knots)
- Range: 944 miles (820 nautical miles, SLAR mission)
- Service ceiling: 25,000 feet
- Rate of climb: 3,450 feet/minute

The Antonov An-124 Ruslan

The Antonov An-124 Ruslan is the world's heaviest gross weight production cargo airplane and second-heaviest operating cargo aircraft, behind the one-off Antonov An-225 Mriya, an enlarged design based on the An-124. The Antonov An-124 remains the largest military transport aircraft in current service.

The first flight took place in December 1982, and the first exposure to the West followed in 1985 at the Paris Air Show.

United Launch Alliance (ULA) contracts the An-124 to transport the Atlas V launch vehicle from its facilities in Decatur, Alabama, to Cape Canaveral. ULA also uses the An-124 to transport the Atlas V launch vehicle and Centaur upper stage from their manufacturing facility in Denver, Colorado, to Cape Canaveral and Vandenberg Air Force Base.

General characteristics
- Crew: Six (pilot, copilot, navigator, senior flight engineer, and a flight engineer and radioman or two loadmasters)
- Capacity: 88 passengers in upper aft fuselage, and the hold can take an additional 350 passengers on a palletized seating system or 330,693 pounds
- Length: 226 feet, 8 inches
- Wing span: 240 feet, 6 inches
- Height: 69 feet, 2 inches

- Wing area: 6,760 square feet
- Aspect ratio: 8.6
- Airfoil: TsAGI supercritical
- Empty weight: 399,037 pounds
- Gross weight: 471,789 pounds maximum fuel weight
- Maximum takeoff weight: 886,258 pounds
- Maximum landing weight: 727,525 pounds
- Fuel capacity: 92,130 US gallons
- Power plant: Four Progress D-18T high-bypass turbofan engines with 51,000-pound thrust each

Performance
- Cruise speed:
  - 537 miles per hour maximum
  - 500 to 530 miles per hour at flight level 328 to 394
- Approach speed: 140 to 160 miles per hour
- Range:
  - 2,300 miles with maximum payload
  - 5,200 miles with 80,000-pound payload
  - 7,100 miles with 88,185-pound payload
- Ferry range: 8,700 miles with maximum fuel and minimum payload
- Service ceiling: 39,000 feet maximum certified altitude
- Wing loading: 131.1 pounds/square foot
- Thrust/weight: 0.23
- Takeoff run (maximum takeoff weight): 9,800 feet
- Landing roll (maximum landing weight): 3,000 feet

The Swearingen Metroliner

The Fairchild Swearingen Metroliner, previously the Swearingen Metro and, later, the Fairchild Aerospace Metro, is a pressurized nineteen-seat twin-turboprop airliner first produced by Swearingen Aircraft and later by Fairchild Aircraft at a plant in San Antonio, Texas. The first flight of the Swearingen Metroliner was on August 26, 1969.

It is a popular aircraft in civilian service, with sales in the nineteen-seat airliner market rivaled only by the Beechcraft 1900. It is especially popular in Australia. Since the first example, a Merlin IVA, arrived in 1975, almost 20 percent of the fleet has operated in that country. As of December 2008, sixty-one Metros and Expediters were registered in Australia, more than all its market rivals combined.

Metro production ended in 1998 when airlines began using regional jets. A total of 703 Metro, Expediter, Merlin IV series, and C-26 series aircraft were built. In addition, 158 other SA226 and SA227 series aircraft were built as short-fuselage Merlin IIIs, IIIAs, and IIIBs.

General characteristics
- Crew: Two (pilot and first officer), or one in cargo-only configuration
- Capacity: 19 passengers or 143.5 cubic feet of cargo
- Length: 59 feet, 4 inches
- Wing span: 57 feet, 0 inches

- Height: 16 feet, 8 inches
- Wing area: 310 square feet
- Empty weight: 8,737 pounds
- Maximum takeoff weight: 14,500 pounds or 16,000 pounds, depending on model
- Power plant: Two Garrett AiResearch TPE331 turboprops with continuous alcohol-water injection and 1,000 shaft horsepower, or 1,100 shaft horsepower with AWI, each
- Propellers: four-bladed McCauley 4HFR34C652 or Dowty Rotol R.321/4-82-F/8

Performance:
- Maximum speed: 311 knots (355 miles per hour)
- Cruise speed: 278 knots (318 miles per hour)
- Range: 684 miles
- Service ceiling: 25,000 feet

The Beechcraft BE-55 Baron

In 1961, Beechcraft introduced the twin-engine Model 55 Baron. The Baron was to be a replacement for the Model 95 Travel Air, which was a bit long in the tooth to meet competition from Cessna's 310 and Piper's Aztec. Like the Travel Air, the Model 55 Baron was comprised of a Beechcraft Bonanza fuselage fitted with a conventional tail, not the V-tail.

In place of the Travel Air's somewhat anemic 180-horsepower Lycoming engines, the original Baron had 260-horsepower Continental IO-470-L engines.

Model 55 Barons were produced from 1961 to 1983, with 3,651 manufactured, including a military version called the T-42A Cochise. The United States Army used the T-42 as an instrument training aircraft as well as officer transportation. By 1993, the army's remaining T-42 aircraft had been transferred to the Army Reserve and the National Guard and were no longer in standard use. Many of those now fly with civilian owners.

More than 6,800 Barons of all variants have been manufactured.

General characteristics
- Crew: One
- Capacity: Five passengers
- Length: 28 feet, 0 inches
- Wing span: 37 feet, 10 inches

- Height: 9 feet, 7 inches
- Wing area: 199.2 square feet
- Airfoil: NACA 23016.5 at root, NACA 23010.5 at tip
- Empty weight: 3,156 pounds
- Maximum takeoff weight: 5,100 pounds
- Fuel capacity: 100 US gallons usable fuel (normal), 136 US gallons with optional tanks
- Power plant: Two Continental IO-470-L air-cooled six-cylinder horizontally opposed engines with 260 horsepower each

Performance
- Maximum speed: 205 knots (236 miles per hour) at sea level
- Cruise speed: 180 knots (210 miles per hour) at 12,000 feet (55 percent power)
- Stall speed: 73 knots (84 miles per hour) indicated airspeed, power off, wheels and flaps lowered
- Range: 942 nautical miles (1,084 miles) at 10,500 feet, 65 percent power, 45-minute reserves
- Service ceiling: 19,700 feet
- Rate of climb: 1,670 feet/minute
- Takeoff distance to 50 feet: 1,675 feet
- Landing distance from 50 feet: 1,840 feet

ACKNOWLEDGMENTS

Thank you to the following:

Spirit of Flight Foundation, Westminster, Colorado, www.spiritofflight.com
Air Assets International, www.airassets.com
Chasing Planes, www.chasingplanestv.com (watch on Amazon Prime)
Robert Collings, www.collingsfoundation.org
Buck Wyndham, www.warbirdalley.com
Legend Flyers and Bob Hammer
www.nbaa.org
www.boeing.com
www.eaa.org
www.mightyeighth.org
www.nwoc.aero
www.gulfstream.com
www.wikipedia.org
www.rockymountainnationalpark.com
www.estes-park.com
www.marcusluttrell.com
www.ada.gov
www.tsa.gov
www.bigginhillheritagehangar.com
www.panam.org
Jane's All the World's Aircraft 2006–2007

Thank you to Dr. Penny Rafferty Hamilton, PhD; Tracey Page; Jim Mills; Celia Morrissey; and Kim Peticolas for all your help.. Thanks to Dr. Gordon West for fixing my broken tooth. Many thanks to all those who have supported me and my mission to save aviation history. Some of the names and destinations in *Seat 29B* have been changed, but the stories are as they happened.

I am sure readers of this book have some crazy stories of their own.

Truth is stranger than fiction.

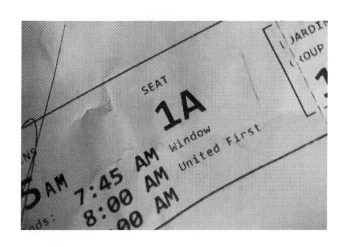